THE POWER OF PERSISTENCE

D1304802

THE POWER OF PERSISTENCE

BREAKTHROUGHS IN YOUR PRAYER LIFE

MICHAEL CATT

NASHVILLE, TENNESSEE

ENDORSEMENTS

This amazing book addresses three critical questions in my personal journey: What is the secret to compassion, creativity, and consistent clarity? How can one church in a small city reach millions through the medium that has eluded our grasp in the past? What is missing today in our denominations and churches across the land? This book, a practical but profound call to prayer, has the answers. If you desire a fresh wind from "elsewhere" to blow away the stale, the shallow, and the status quo, then discover *The Power of Persistence*.

    —Jay Strack, President
    Student Leadership University

Some men write on subjects their research has prompted, while others feel the need to address the passion of their lives and ministry. The latter serves as the inspiration of this book, as its subject of prayer has been fleshed out in the life of its author. This is a must-read for anyone who desires intimacy through persistence in prayer.

    —Johnny Hunt, Senior Pastor
    First Baptist Church, Woodstock, Georgia
    President, Southern Baptist Convention

Aristotle said, "Give me a place to stand, and I can move the world." Michael's book really nails it. It tells me how to get to that place on my knees before the throne and stay there until it happens. And it *will* happen.

    —John Bisagno, Senior Pastor
    Colonial Heights Baptist Church
    Ridgeland, Mississippi

We need this book today more than ever, not because people won't fill our churches even when we are spiritually empty. We need this book today because a sovereign God has inextricably linked the persistent praying of His people to the manifestation of His life-changing power and sin-killing presence. The old, old story told by prayed-up preachers who are leading prayed-up churches still works. It's the only thing that really works.

—**Alan Day, Senior Pastor**
Edmond's First Baptist Church, Edmond, Oklahoma

This book is a compelling challenge to move to the next level in our Christian walk. It is powerful because it is personal. Michael has been a part of every major event in my life and the life of my family through his consistent prayer for us. This book and Michael's example have made a significant impact in my life.

—**Charles S. Lowery**
Lowery Institute of Excellence

If you want to know how to get from where you are to where you want to be, the book you hold in your hand will show you the way. Discover the intimacy of speaking to the King in the King's own language as Michael Catt teaches you how to pray the Word in a powerful and effective way. When you do, your life will never be the same!

—**Kerry Shook, Senior Pastor**
Woodlands Church, The Woodlands, Texas

Get hold of prayer and experience a depth with God you've never known before. Dig into Michael Catt's powerful work and be amazed at what God can do in you.

—**James MacDonald, Senior Pastor**
Harvest Bible Chapel, Rolling Meadows, Illinois

TABLE OF CONTENTS

DEDICATION

DON AND LIBBY MILLER: Prayer warriors who first introduced me to the necessity of an intercessory prayer ministry in the local church. They have traveled this nation for decades teaching churches to pray. No one taught me more about the church being a "house of prayer" than Don. Meeting them in 1985 was a divine appointment.

ROGER AND LINDA BRELAND: Friends for nearly forty years. They have prayed for me, my family, and my ministry like no others. Linda is the greatest prayer warrior I have ever met. Their lives are a testimony to the power of prayer and faith.

JAMES MILLER: My youth minister growing up who started youth prayer meetings during the days of the Jesus Movement. We didn't have a budget, camps, or retreats, but we learned that prayer is the key to God working among His people.

FOREWORD

Is your "spiritual address" in Jerusalem, or in Athens? And in which city is the church located where you worship and serve?

Christians who live in Athens spend their time "doing nothing but talking about and listening to the latest ideas" (Acts 17:21 NIV). These religious novelties entertain them for a short time, but they don't produce the kind of ministry that glorifies Jesus Christ and transforms lives. Religious entertainment may build a crowd, but that isn't the same as spiritual edification that builds a church.

Mature Christians know the difference. Believers who live in Jerusalem follow the time-honored biblical discipline of giving their attention to "prayer and the ministry of the word" (Acts 6:4 NIV). The first Christians didn't have to search around for some "new thing," because they got it right the first time—"prayer and the ministry of the word." The Athens approach may look attractive, but the Jerusalem approach is spiritually effective, and it produces fruit that lasts. "I urge, then, first of all, that requests, prayers, intercession and thanksgiving be made for everyone," wrote Paul (1 Tim. 2:1 NIV). Prayer first! This is not an option; it's an obligation.

During my years of itinerant ministry, I have found here and there pastors and churches who prefer the apostolic approach to the Athenian approach—and Sherwood Baptist Church in Albany, Georgia, is one of those churches. When I have stood before that congregation to share the Word, I have sensed the Holy Spirit at work because the congregation and staff had prayed. Their senior pastor, Michael Catt, as well as the church staff and officers, agree with Paul that prayer and the preaching of the Word of God must have priority.

In this book Pastor Catt builds a biblical base for praying churches and praying church leaders, a case it is impossible to refute. It warmed and stirred my heart to read these chapters, and I trust you will have the same experience. I suggest you share this book with some of your friends. This might give birth to a vibrant prayer group in your neighborhood or church. "For the person who knows to do good and doesn't do it, it is a sin" (James 4:17).

God bless you in exercising your prayer privileges as a citizen of that glorious heavenly Jerusalem (Heb. 12:18–24).

— **Warren W. Wiersbe**

INTRODUCTION

When we work, we work. But when we pray, God works.

Everything good in my life and in the life of the church I pastor, I attribute to praying people. Every blessing has come from a prayer environment. Every time I've seen Satan win the day, I know we've let our prayer guard down. And every time we've moved forward as a church family, it has been on our knees.

I've had two great things happen in my life that led me to understand the significance of persistent praying. The first was as a young person. We had prayer meetings in my home church where I learned the value of intercession. I learned by doing, by believing God to save the lost, deliver the captives, and meet impossible needs.

The second was while serving at Sagamore Hill Baptist Church in Fort Worth, Texas. Don Miller, one of the greatest prayer warriors I've ever met, was a member. Not long after I moved there, he did a prayer seminar for the church. I saw in Don Miller the power of a praying life. Because of his influence, I began to understand the significance and necessity of an Intercessory Prayer Ministry in the local church.

Today I am privileged to pastor a church with a 24/7 intercessory prayer ministry. Most of the churches I served in my ministry did not have this sort of deliberate emphasis. Oh, we prayed for the sick and for the things we felt obligated to, but we didn't have a focused prayer ministry. We had prayer meeting on Wednesday nights, but I rarely remember us praying for anything or anyone other than physically sick people. There's nothing wrong with that, but the spiritually sick and lost were largely ignored. Ingrown toenails were more important than drug addicts and prodigals.

Much has been said about our church in recent years. The stories of Sherwood Pictures in particular, including our successful films *Flywheel*, *Facing the Giants*, and *Fireproof*, have made national news. In 2007, the *Facing the Giants* DVD was the number-one seller among all products in Christian bookstores except for the Bible. We've been featured in national media outlets, both secular and Christian, including *Dr. Phil*, the front page of the *Los Angeles Times*, Focus on the Family, and many more.

We are often asked why God has blessed us in this way. The answer is simple. We have a praying church that is walking in unity. We pray over every ministry and every decision that affects how we "reach the world from Albany, Georgia."

In recent years we've focused on this truth: whoever wants the next generation the most will get them. I want to see the church militant, aggressive, passionate, and revived. It will not happen apart from prayer and unity.

I am the pastor of this church as a direct result of the pulpit committee calling the church to prayer. I had turned down the committee chairman three times. I wasn't interested in moving to Georgia, but God turned my heart. I believe it was because of praying people who sought God's will and God's man. I didn't *know* I was God's man. Neither did they. But in prayer, God put us together. This year we will celebrate twenty years as pastor and people, and the only reason we've survived our "many dangers, toils, and snares" is because of prayer.

We have seen God expand our borders through prayer. Today we reach twenty-nine communities surrounding the city of Albany. Some of our members drive more than forty miles one-way to get here. We have an eighty-two-acre sports park featuring a 110-foot cross, an area that has been thoroughly and often prayed over. In the near future we plan to build a rock base around the cross to hold a container filled with thousands of prayer cards written for the people who will walk on that property. It is our prayer that we can use sports as a means of evangelism and building relationships in our community.

We have a prayer chapel on our high school campus and a two-story prayer tower at the front of the church. We have nearly two hundred men who have committed to being what we call "pastor's prayer partners." They take turns coming on Sunday mornings to our worship center to pray over the services held there. Spurgeon's Prayer Room is located under our choir loft where people gather and pray during the morning and evening services.

Every year before our ReFRESH™ Conference, we have a week of intensive prayer for revival. Our people place the names of loved ones and personal needs on the altar as we ask God to do the miraculous in seemingly impossible situations.

I know there is not a day that goes by when members of this church are not praying for me. I have friends in the ministry who pray for me every day. It makes me want to be better—to do more, serve Jesus more, pray more, and study more. It makes me realize how desperately I need the intercessions of others to do what God has called me to do. My ministry is not a one-way street where I minister only to others; it is a two-way street where people minister to me, especially through prayer.

People have prayed for me as I've been writing this book. People have prayed for me in times of personal crisis and loss. People have prayed when the enemy sought to attack us from without as well as from within. Partnering in prayer is not a new concept. In fact, it is as old as the Word of God. Moses prayed for Joshua as he battled in the valley. The disciples gathered in an upper room to pray for power, then Peter preached and three thousand were converted. Partnering in prayer also has deep roots in the history of well-known pastors and missionaries:

- Charles Finney: Rochester, New York, 1830—In one year, one thousand of the city's ten thousand citizens came to faith in Christ. Abel Clary was Finney's prayer partner.

Finney wrote of him, "Mr. Clary continued as long as I did and did not leave until after I had left. He never appeared in public, but gave himself wholly to prayer."

- D. L. Moody: London, England, 1872—A bedridden girl named Marianne Adlard had read a clipping about Moody and prayed that God would send him to her church. Within ten days, four hundred new converts came into the church where he was preaching.

- Jonathan Goforth, Canadian missionary: Manchuria, China, 1909—Great revival and awakening had been occurring during Goforth's ministry in China. While in London later that year, he was taken to see an invalid lady. As they talked about the revival, she asked him to look at her notebook. She had recorded three days when special power came upon her for his meetings in Manchuria. These were the very same days that he witnessed the greatest evidences of God's power there.

- Mordecai Ham, revivalist: Charlotte, North Carolina, 1934—Several businessmen, along with Billy Graham's father, spent a day at the family farm praying that God would touch their city, their state, and their world through Dr. Ham's meeting in Charlotte. During one of the revival services, Billy Graham came to Christ.

- Billy Graham: Los Angeles, California, 1949—An extended campaign resulted in a new era of mass evangelism. Graham said the only difference between the meeting in L.A. and previous meetings was the amount of prayer the team put into this one meeting.

- John Wesley said, "Give me a hundred preachers who fear nothing but sin and desire nothing but God, and I care not a straw whether they be clergy or laymen. Such alone will shake the gates of hell and set up the kingdom of Heaven on earth. God does nothing but in answer to prayer."
- C. H. Spurgeon said, "Whenever God determines to do a great work, He first sets His people to pray." He attributed the success of his sermons not to his photographic memory, his keen intellect, or his powerful preaching. He said it was "the prayers of an illiterate lay brother who sat on the pulpit steps pleading for the success of the sermons."

I was pastoring the First Baptist Church of Ada, Oklahoma, in 1988 when Don Miller came there to do a prayer conference. One day during the conference, we had eighteen inches of snow. I asked Don if he wanted to cancel the evening sessions. He told me that people who were serious about prayer would make their way through the snow to attend. And, yes, despite eighteen inches of snow—with the rest of the town completely shut down—150 people showed up at the church for the conference. That was a night I will never forget!

When we pray, we partner with the supernatural. We change the ordinary to the extraordinary and the mundane to the miraculous. I am in no way an expert on prayer. I feel like my prayer life is anemic compared to prayer warriors I know. I can't write from an expert's perspective, but I can write of what God has taught me about the power of persistent praying and the power of a praying church. As you read this book, I pray that God will move you to become an intercessor. I pray that He will use this book to encourage pastors and lay people to start intercessory prayer ministries in their churches. It is my hope that all of us will learn that prayer is on the cutting edge of every work of God.

The ups and downs of church history can be written in the prayer life of God's people. The strength of the church has never been in programs, numbers, or events, but in prayer and obedience. God is not interested in our innovative methods. He is not impressed with our twenty-first century technology. God is still moved by the prayers of simple saints who learn in the quiet place to lay hold of the throne of grace. Prayer is not incidental to the work of God—it *is* the work!

— **Michael Catt**

CHAPTER 1

THE PROPHETIC AND PROFITABLE WORK OF PRAYER

1 Kings 17–18

Prayer honours God, acknowledges his being, exalts his power, adores his providence, secures his aid.
—E. M. Bounds

Rejoice always! Pray constantly. Give thanks in everything, for this is God's will for you in Christ Jesus.
—1 Thessalonians 5:16–18

MOST OF US are familiar with the Old Testament prophet Elijah. We know the story of his battle on Mount Carmel, but I think we often overlook the significance of his prayer life. The battles in Elijah's life were won through prayer. Prayer is the most profitable work any person can do. It pays dividends that cannot be put into words or measured in a ledger.

When you think about many believers, the last word that comes to mind when describing their prayer life is power. Yet prayer is the key to the throne of heaven; it is the secret to power and access to the throne of grace. In prayer, we partner with the Holy Spirit who is, even right now, praying with our Lord Jesus and interceding for us at the right hand of the Father. This fact alone should infuse our prayer life with power. Right?

Then why doesn't it?

I think of it this way. Our house has separate air conditioning and heating units, one that operates on half the house and one on the other. On a cold morning not long ago, I walked to the other side of the house and found it was freezing. I pushed the thermostat up warmer, but nothing happened. At that point I knew that either the heater was broken or a circuit had been blown. How did I know? Because the hall light was on. Obviously we had available electricity on that side of the house, but no power for the heater.

Isn't this our problem in prayer? We have available power, but it doesn't seem to be working in us or through us. Our churches are powerless because they are prayerless. We generally do a lot more *worrying* on our knees than praying, then we get up and continue to worry.

Where is the power that can call down fire from heaven? Where are the kinds of prayers that lead to divine intervention? It's not that God's heart is cold; it's that we have forgotten what God is looking for. If I am not walking in power, the problem is with me, not with God. If I am living in fear of the forces of evil, it is because I lack confidence that God will show Himself in power.

I believe one reason Elijah was chosen to represent the prophets on the Mount of Transfiguration is that he was a powerful man of prayer. Think about how significant Elijah is, even in the New Testament. He represents the high water mark of the prophets. When John the Baptist came, he was said to be like Elijah. When Jesus asked, "Who do men say that I am?" some said, "Elijah."

The New Testament does not present him as a superhero but as a man just like us. Therefore, Elijah knew something about prayer that we can know. He had the kind of prayer life we too can have. Here's the key: he faced his problems and opportunities in believing prayer. He believed God was his source and resource. Maybe the reason we don't receive answers to many prayers is we really don't expect God to answer. We might kneel down, say a few words, and quote a Scripture, but in truth—in our hearts—we don't believe anything is going to change.

Not Elijah.

BELIEVE IT OR NOT?

Elijah lived in a godless time. If he were to arrive on the scene today, he would not be shocked by our culture. Idolatry, sensuality, corruption, and godlessness were rampant. He lived in the day when Ahab was king of Israel. Ahab and Queen Jezebel would make some of today's corrupt politicians look like Mr. Rogers. They introduced Baal worship and even built a temple to Baal in Samaria.

When God's people face godless times, that's when they need to turn up the heat in prayer. Tough times are no time for God's people to sit by, cold and indifferent. As you read 1 Kings, you will discover that before the showdown on Mount Carmel, God was preparing Elijah in prayer. Elijah was learning how to ask God for the impossible and believe God in desperate situations. Before he ever stood on Carmel and confronted the false prophets, Elijah was a man of prayer and faith in the promises of God. All of us must be tested as to whether we will take matters into our own hands or take them before the Lord. Read how Elijah did it in 1 Kings 17:8–24.

> The word of the LORD came to him: "Get up, go to Zarephath that belongs to Sidon, and stay there. Look, I have commanded a woman who is a widow to provide for you there." So Elijah got up and went to Zarephath. When he arrived at the city gate, there was a widow woman gathering wood. Elijah called to her and said, "Please bring me a little water in a cup and let me drink." As she went to get it, he called to her and said, "Please bring me a piece of bread in your hand."

But she said, "As the LORD your God lives, I don't have anything baked—only a handful of flour in the jar and a bit of oil in the jug. Just now, I am gathering a couple of sticks in order to go prepare it for myself and my son so we can eat it and die."

Then Elijah said to her, "Don't be afraid; go and do as you have said. Only make me a small loaf from it and bring it out to me. Afterwards, you may make some for yourself and your son, for this is what the LORD God of Israel says: 'The flour jar will not become empty and the oil jug will not run dry until the day the LORD sends rain on the surface of the land.'"

So she proceeded to do according to the word of Elijah. She and he and her household ate for many days. The flour jar did not become empty, and the oil jug did not run dry, according to the word of the LORD He had spoken through Elijah.

After this, the son of the woman who owned the house became ill. His illness became very severe until no breath remained in him. She said to Elijah, "Man of God, what do we have in common? Have you come to remind me of my guilt and to kill my son?"

But Elijah said to her, "Give me your son." So he took him from her arms, brought him up to the upper room where he was staying, and laid him on his own bed. Then he cried out to the LORD and said, "My LORD God, have You also brought tragedy on the widow I am stay-ing with by killing her son?" Then he stretched himself out over the boy three times. He cried out to the LORD and said, "My LORD God, please let this boy's life return to him!"

So the LORD listened to Elijah's voice, and the boy's life returned to him, and he lived. Then Elijah took the boy, brought him down from the upper room into the house, and gave him to his mother. Elijah said, "Look, your son is alive." Then the woman said to Elijah, "Now I know you are a man of God and the LORD's word in your mouth is the truth.

Here you see clearly that powerful praying is tied to the Word of God. We can believe what God has revealed in His Word. Elijah, in communion with God, was able to see a power working through his life that was not available otherwise.

If Elijah had followed the normal pattern, he would have said, "Lord, comfort this woman in her grief." Instead, he asked God to raise the boy from the dead! This is an incredible request, a bold request in light of the fact that no one in recorded his-tory had ever been raised from the dead.

Powerful praying begins with believing God to be our pro-vision. Elijah had seen God protect him and provide for him through the drought and famine. He knew that if God could provide for him in the wilderness, He could provide for this widow in the city. When he met the widow gathering sticks, she thought it was near the end. Elijah arrived to show her it's not over until God says it's over.

Because God had taught Elijah to trust Him for provision as Jehovah Jireh—"God who provides"—it was nothing for him to first challenge the widow to trust God's power for her provisions and then to trust God for her son. Elijah had a big view of God. Our tendency is to have a big view of our situations and a small view of God's sovereignty. We tend to see God through a microscope and our problems through a telescope, but it should be the other way around. Our problems are miniscule compared to the vastness of God.

Prayer is faith acting like it's supposed to act. Elijah "stretched himself out over the boy three times." Not once. Not twice. Powerful praying demands discipline and patience. God is not a bellhop who comes running at the snap of our fingers. God wants us to stretch ourselves in the realm of prayer. When is the last time you asked God for something you couldn't figure out?

Several years ago we had a specific season of prayer for impossible circumstances. We asked our church members to fill out a prayer card and list three impossible (or as we called them, HIMpossible) situations in their personal lives or family. They laid the cards on the altar, and for forty days we covered those requests in prayer. Some of the requests were seemingly impossible, far beyond anyone's ability to orchestrate.

During those forty days, several couples who were dealing with infertility miraculously conceived children. We heard of people experiencing dramatic transformations in their families. We saw prodigals come home. We witnessed the salvation of family members. God took the impossible and turned it into a HIMpossible.

As I have written in my book *The Power of Desperation*, we have seen miracles. How sad that we often attribute miracles only to biblical times. No, I don't believe in "name it, claim it" theology. I don't believe that healing is part of the atonement. But I do believe we are to pray and seek and ask and knock and trust God with the results. God may, in fact, be more willing to work than we are willing to pray.

WHEN'S THE LAST TIME YOU ASKED GOD FOR SOMETHING THAT WAS BEYOND YOUR ABILITY?

Was everyone's prayer answered? No. We're still waiting on some of the answers. At one of our ReFRESH™ Conferences, someone placed a family member's name on the altar. Two years later that initial prayer was answered in a powerful and dramatic way.

When's the last time you asked God for something that was beyond your ability? When did you last approach the throne of grace with confidence for something you couldn't figure out or take credit for? Have you stopped trusting Him to save people? Have you given up on impossible situations?

Jesus raised the dead, healed the sick, and opened blind eyes with a word or a touch. But it cost Him His life to pay our penalty of sin and death. However, I can pray for my lost friends and family members because He died so that they might live. It's not up to me to determine their response. It is up to me to intercede and believe that God has the power to change hearts.

Elijah went places in his intercession no one had gone before. There is no indication he was hesitant to ask for these things. There seems to be no doubt in his mind that God could do it. Notice that the mother wasn't with Elijah when he prayed for her son. This kind of prevailing, powerful intercession is not a group exercise—it is done alone with God in the secret place. Elijah's prayer was directed to God because the issue was God's to decide. Elijah knew this had to be a God thing. The prophet had no authority over death, but God did.

FIRE ON THE MOUNTAIN

Elijah is on Mount Carmel the next time we see him praying. There's a battle at hand between Elijah and the prophets of Baal. He proposed that two altars be set up on the mountain, one for Baal and one for God. The prophets of Baal would pray and then Elijah would pray. The god who answered by fire would be the true God.

The false prophets jumped up and down, cut themselves, and cried out to Baal all day long, but nothing happened. Then Elijah set up his altar, poured water over it to make it even harder to ignite, and said a brief prayer.

At the time for offering the evening sacrifice, Elijah the prophet approached the altar and said, "LORD God of Abraham, Isaac, and Israel, today let it be known that You are God in Israel and I am Your servant, and that at Your word I have done all these things. Answer me, LORD! Answer me so that this people will know that You, Yahweh, are God and that You have turned their hearts back." Then Yahweh's fire fell and consumed the burnt offering, the wood, the stones, and the dust, and it licked up the water that was in the trench. When all the people saw it, they fell facedown and said, "Yahweh, He is God! Yahweh, He is God!" (1 Kings 18:36–39)

There are several truths I do not want you to miss. *First, this was a show of power.* Israel had bought the lie that Baal had power, and they put their faith in idols. They needed a lesson from the God of Abraham, Isaac, and Jacob. They needed a reminder that the one true God delivered the people out of bondage, across the Red Sea, and into the Promised Land. Jehovah was not a distant deity, nor was He a symbol or a statue. He was the living Lord. He had clearly stated, "You shall have no other gods before Me."

Secondly, Elijah tied obedience to power. He wasn't afraid to be identified with the Lord God of Israel. He was outnumbered, but he wasn't outgunned. He was unashamed of the Lord, willing to hitch his wagon, his future, and even his life to God's ability and power to intervene.

Thirdly, he was confident God would hear and act. Elijah didn't pray with a wavering faith; he believed God. He soaked the altar so there would be no doubt as to God's ability to do exceedingly, abundantly beyond what he ever hoped or imagined.

The false prophets and the people of Israel believed Baal was the god who controlled the weather. Unfortunately the people had forgotten their history. The God of Israel was able to send manna from heaven and bring forth water from a rock. Over and over throughout their history God had shown His power to rule and overrule the laws of nature. Yet they couldn't decide. They halted between two opinions. They weren't willing to believe God.

Doesn't that still happen today? We fail to believe in God and His ability to provide because we trust in ourselves and our own abilities. No, we don't have Baals in our houses or altars to Asherah in our yards, but we give evidence daily that we don't believe God has the power to meet us at the point of our need. We trust in our ability to work and make a living. We live on two incomes because we need them to "get by." We fail to tithe because we don't believe God has the power to do what He says He will do for those who obey His Word regarding tithing and giving.

Why was such a demonstration needed? Why such a big show? Why not just deal with Ahab one-on-one and forget this? What if God didn't show up? What if neither God nor Baal could answer?

God *was* going to answer, but the people needed to see for themselves the futility of idolatry. These false prophets prayed, but they had no power. They went to extremes, but their god did nothing. Their gods were false with no power or ability because they were empty and incapable.

Finally, the nation needed to turn back to God. While it is always encouraging to see God move here and there, the longing of my heart is to see God move again across this land. We are in desperate need of revival to sweep our nation. But it will not come if we are hesitant or content with business as usual. It only comes to those who see the need and ask the God who can part the sea, raise the dead, heal the sick, and feed the multitudes to once again show Himself in power.

Much like the day in which we live, Elijah lived in a backslidden nation. The laws of God had been forgotten, and His miracles were a distant memory. The nation was in a spiritual and physical drought, desperately needing a fire to burn away the dross—living water to quench their thirsty hearts. They had been drinking from broken cisterns that could not even hold water. The nation faced judgment, and only the intervention of the power of God could change things.

I wonder, where are the Christians, the churches, that are believing God for revival? Where are those who long to see God move as He did in days past? Are we so entrenched that we cannot wake ourselves from our lethargy and seek once again the power from on high? Elijah didn't pray so that people would think he was a great prophet or talk about his power. He didn't pray in order for his church to grow. He asked God to answer him so the people would know that the Lord was Yahweh, the Lord God.

The power and fire of God will fall on His people when three things happen:

1) When we are willing to serve God with our whole heart. "How long will you hesitate between two opinions? If Yahweh is God, follow Him. But if Baal, follow him" (1 Kings 18:21).

2) When we think more about the glory of God than our personal safety and take our stand with God before this pagan world.

3) When we are willing to believe God and do something about it.

LET IT RAIN

I once read the story of a man who stood at the grave of John Wesley. Wesley's preaching, as you probably know, was one of the deterrents that saved England from a civil war. He shook a nation. His work led to a national revival. As the man stood at Wesley's tombstone, he prayed, "Do it again, Lord, do it again."

I can remember times when I've stood at the graves of men like Vance Havner and Ron Dunn, both great men of prayer and faith, and asked God to use me as an instrument of revival. God wants to work. I believe he's looking for a body, a remnant, a prophet, or a preacher whom He can trust with that work.

I was privileged in 2008 to serve as president of the Southern Baptist Convention Pastors' Conference. The theme of the conference was "Prepare for Rain," and the four sessions followed what I believe to be the path to biblical revival and power. The first session dealt with *prayer*. We cannot go any further until we resolve that prayer is a key to all we do and say. The next session focused on *brokenness*. As we pray, we are broken by our sin of apathy, the sins of others, and the sins of the nation. Brokenness is the "woe is me" before we can say, "God, use me." Then we looked at *revival*, a fresh movement of God resulting from our brokenness. Following revival, there is historically a great move of *evangelism*, so we finished the conference with this emphasis. Revival must come before evangelism. We will lack power in our missions and evangelism if there is not a move of revival. Carnal people do not care for lost people.

I began the conference by asking the pastors, staff members, and others assembled to listen to these fourteen men who would be preaching—to listen the way they'd want their own people to listen when *they* preached. And yet while the conference was going on, I saw men reading newspapers, talking to one another, sending text messages, even roaming around the room as if nothing was happening. During the invitation of one session, hundreds got up to beat the crowd to the meal.

This is why we have no power: we have no respect for God. If we as preachers can't get it right, how can we expect our churches to get it right?

I am grateful, of course, that these illustrations represented only a small minority. The overwhelming majority of those who came to the Pastors' Conference were tuned in. At the end of the prayer session, hundreds upon hundreds came to the front to seek the Lord. Many were on their faces on the concrete floor. Some cried. Others stretched out as if trying to touch heaven.

During the four sessions of the conference, we gave three such invitations. Never to my knowledge had we ever given so many invitations during this type of conference. I firmly believe God laid it on my heart to call us back to prayer. Our convention is dying. Other denominations are dying. Baptisms are down. Darkness is invading the land. Surely we can admit that we are powerless primarily because we are prayerless.

> **A POWERFUL PRAYER IS ONE THAT DOES NOT LET GO. IT DOES NOT QUIT.**

But all is not lost. Not all have given up. I well recall one afternoon session when a major thunderstorm had begun brewing, severe enough to cause road closings and flash flooding, delaying some of the people who were traveling in. But God was speaking to the heart of one particular man in attendance, who was specifically asking the Lord to "rain down" on his life and ministry. He made his way to the front of the stage during the invitation. Soon the ceiling right above his head began to leak, and rain started dripping on him. He said to himself, "I can either get up and get away from this leak, or I can lie here and see it as a sign from God." He stayed there and got soaked.

Oh, let it rain! Do it again, Lord!

KEEP ON KEEPING ON

A powerful prayer is one that does not let go. It does not quit. It is profitable and powerful because it is persistent. I consider the following passage to be the greatest story in Scripture on the power of prevailing prayer.

Elijah said to Ahab, "Go up, eat and drink; for there is the sound of a rainstorm." So Ahab went to eat and drink, but Elijah went up to the summit of Carmel. He bowed down to the ground and put his face between his knees. Then he said to his servant, "Go up and look toward the sea." So he went up, looked, and said, "There's nothing." Seven times Elijah said, "Go back." On the seventh time, he reported, "There's a cloud as small as a man's hand coming from the sea." Then Elijah said, "Go and tell Ahab, 'Get your chariot ready and go down so the rain doesn't stop you.'" In a little while, the sky grew dark with clouds and wind, and there was a downpour. So Ahab got in his chariot and went to Jezreel. The power of the LORD was on Elijah, and he tucked his mantle under his belt and ran ahead of Ahab to the entrance of Jezreel. (1 Kings 18:41–46)

Three years before, Elijah had prayed for the rain to stop as a sign of judgment. Now it was time to pray for rain again because judgment had been rendered. When Elijah went to pray, he wasn't hoping, he was expecting. He was watching and waiting for God's answer. Note that Elijah never interpreted the delay as denial from God. He called out seven times before there was the slightest indication that rain was coming. Six times he heard, "There is nothing." Yet he never quit praying.

Throughout the Old and New Testaments, we are reminded to persist in prayer until God breaks through.

> I will not keep silent because of Zion, and I will not keep still because of Jerusalem until her righteousness shines like a bright light, and her salvation like a flaming torch. . . . I have appointed watchmen on your walls; they will never be silent, day or night. You, who remind the LORD, no rest for you! Do not give Him rest until He establishes and makes her Jerusalem the praise of the earth. (Isa. 62:1, 6–7)

> He then told them a parable on the need for them to pray always and not become discouraged. (Luke 18:1)

> Devote yourselves to prayer; stay alert in it with thanksgiving. (Col. 4:2)

> Rejoice always! Pray constantly. Give thanks in everything, for this is God's will for you in Christ Jesus. (1 Thess. 5:16–18)

We also have the accounts of other Christians who have believed God in persistent prayer. George Mueller prayed sixty-three years for the salvation of a friend, who finally gave his heart to Christ at Mueller's funeral. C. H. Spurgeon said:

> If you are sure it is a right thing for which you are asking, plead now, plead at noon, plead at night, plead on. With cries and tears spread out your case. Order your arguments. Back up your pleas with reasons. Urge the precious blood of Jesus. Bring out the atoning sacrifice. Point to Calvary. Enlist the Priest who stands at the right hand of God. And resolve in your very soul that if souls be not saved, if your family be not blessed, if your own zeal be not revived, yet you will die with the plea on your lips, and with the appealing wish on your spirits.[1]

There had not been a drop of rain in Israel for three and a half years, but Elijah prayed nonetheless. James writes, "Elijah was a man with a nature like ours; yet he prayed earnestly that it would not rain, and for three years and six months it did not rain on the land. Then he prayed again, and the sky gave rain and the land produced its fruit" (5:17–18). According to James, Elijah was a man just like us. But the question comes: Are we men just like him? I read the stories of prayer warriors and find I have far to go. I probably have no business writing a book on prayer. Based on prayer warriors I know, I'm still a novice. When I hear some people who get hold of God, I wonder if I've ever said anything in my prayers.

I have read, for example, of John "Praying" Hyde, who arrived in England in April 1911 to begin praying for the work of Dr. Wilbur Chapman, who was leading a series of meetings there. They had experienced much resistance and little fruit or evidence of power thus far. Chapman said he received a note about Hyde coming to intercede and wrote, "Almost instantly the tide turned. The hall was packed, and my first invitation meant fifty men for Jesus Christ. As we were leaving I said, 'Mr. Hyde, I want you to pray for me.' He came to my room, turned the key to the door and dropped to his knees."

Five minutes passed without a single word uttered. Then Hyde looked toward heaven with tears streaming down his face and said, "O, God!" followed by another five minutes without a word being spoken. Finally, Chapman said, "He began to pray as I have never heard before. I rose from my knees knowing what real prayer is."

IT COULD BE YOU

James begins and ends his epistle with a call to prayer, presenting Elijah as the poster child for it, holding up this one specific person as an example of how to pray. The book of James is filled with references to prayer—prayer in the midst of trials, prayer when you lack wisdom, and so on. Someone has said, "Faith's finest work is when believers are effective in prayer."

In James 4 we are reminded to draw near to God. Then in James 5 he tells us who to pray for and how to pray. He tells us to pray in problems, in pleasure, and in pain. "Therefore, confess your sins to one another and pray for one another, so that you may be healed. The intense prayer of the righteous is very powerful" (5:16). Effective praying is specific praying that has specific results in mind. It's far more than merely, "Bless those for whom it is our duty to pray." It means a humble, begging plea. It's a picture of someone asking God for help, not demanding it, but approaching heaven with integrity in prayer and intensity in their intercession. Elijah is our example. He prayed earnestly, which literally means he "prayed in his prayers." He didn't just spout off high-sounding words. He didn't try to impress God with what he was saying.

> Elijah was human, a follower of God who sometimes got depressed or had doubts. He snatched defeat out of the jaws of victory when he ran from Jezebel after decisively crushing the prophets of Baal. But James uses Elijah as an example of someone who did not allow his own weaknesses to undermine his trust in God. Elijah's weak belief in himself forced him to believe even more firmly in God. James is inviting us to identify with Elijah's weakness so that we might develop the same honesty and power in prayer that Elijah exercised. The same God who listened to and acted on Elijah's prayers will give attention to ours."[2]

Jesus made an incredible promise in the gospel of John: "I assure you: The one who believes in Me will also do the works that I do. And he will do even greater works than these, because I am going to the Father" (14:12). He talks about works and greater works. Would you agree that "greater works" would be powerful and profitable witnesses in these cynical days? Jesus would soon ascend into heaven, and the Spirit would come to live within His disciples. He tried to teach His followers that the life of believing prayer would result in a life that bore fruit. Ron Dunn, in his book on prayer, writes of four truths we need to learn from the teachings of Jesus on prayer.

1) When Jesus encourages us to pray He always uses limitless language. ("Whatever you ask," "Ask, seek, knock"—don't pray as if God has declared bankruptcy.)

2) Jesus reminds us to ask in His name. ("Whatever you ask in My name"—according to His character, to honor His name.)

3) Jesus reminds us He Himself is the answer. (He didn't say, "I'll give you advice," or "I will help you." He said, "I will do it." Many of our prayers are limited because we limit in our minds what we think God can do.)

4) Jesus assures us He will answer. ("That the Father may be glorified in the Son"—the motive behind our asking is the glory of God.)

Ron often shared the following story in Bible conferences. The church he was pastoring had a pancake sale to raise $4,000 for a youth choir tour. Located next to the church was a Whataburger, a popular fast food restaurant in Texas. One Saturday, the church was covered with signs and looked like a carnival. Deacons were wearing hats that read "Whatapancake." People were cooking and selling pancakes left and right. They raised $2,000. The following Wednesday night, Ron told the church that as long as he was pastor, they would never again have a sale to raise money. They were going to trust God to meet their needs, and they were going to believe God for the other $2,000.

Later in the week a young lady who had been married only three months called Ron. She and her newlywed husband were barely getting by, but she had recently been in a car accident and the insurance company had settled her claim at $3,000. She still had $2,000 of it in a savings account and felt God wanted her to give it to the youth choir tour. Ron said, "We raised $2,000 by pancakes and $2,000 by prayer. After we sold pancakes, I thanked everyone who had a part in the fund-raiser and then worried that I might have forgotten somebody. When we raised $2,000 by prayer, we just thanked the Lord and He got all the glory."

I wonder how much praying we really do in the church. We *say* we pray, but we mainly just ask God to bless our fleshly efforts. We pray for the Lord to help us make the batter and sell the pancakes. The truth is that God wants us to trust Him and get out of the pancake business.

I mentioned John Hyde earlier. Better known as "Praying" Hyde, he was born in Illinois in 1865, the son of a Presbyterian minister. He had heard the call to missions early on and had journeyed to India, where the natives referred to him as "the man who never sleeps." He often spent thirty days and nights in prayer, many times staying on his knees in deep intercession for thirty-six hours at a time.

His prayer life spilled over into his work, which was mightily blessed of God in India, proving both powerful and spiritually profitable. Although he is known for his prayer life—some have called him the "apostle of prayer"—it is said that Hyde typically won four to ten people a day to saving faith in Jesus Christ. He died on February 17, 1912. His last words were, "Shout the victory of Jesus Christ!"

One of my favorite books is Raymond Edman's *They Found the Secret: Twenty Transformed Lives That Reveal a Touch of Eternity*. I still own the copy I bought as a young preacher. Although the spine is broken, the truths within are still as real today as ever. In one chapter Edman writes about John Hyde and the prevailing life:

> It is recorded that . . . John Hyde gave himself to much prayer . . . praying that he might indeed be filled with the Spirit and know by actual experience what Jesus meant when He said: "Ye shall receive power, when the Holy Ghost is coming upon you; and ye shall be my witnesses both in Jerusalem, and in all Judea and Samaria, and unto the uttermost part of the earth."
>
> In 1904 a group of missionaries, inspired by Hyde's prayer life, formed the Punjab Prayer Union. Those becoming members were required to sign these five simple yet searching principles:

1) Are you praying for quickening in your own life, in the life of your fellow workers, and in the church?

2) Are you longing for greater power of the Holy Spirit in your own life and work, and are you convinced that you cannot go on without this power?

3) Will you pray that you may not be ashamed of Jesus?

4) Do you believe that prayer is the great means of securing this spiritual awakening?

5) Will you set apart one-half hour each day as soon after noon as possible to pray for this awakening, and are you willing to pray till the awakening comes?

It is difficult to measure the impact and importance of Hyde's service that came as a result of his Spirit-filled prayer life.[3]

Once Hyde was asked to preach at a conference and arrived late. When he stood to preach, he said, "I did not sleep any last night, and I have not eaten anything today. I have been having a controversy with God. I feel that He has warned me to come here and testify to you concerning some things that He has done for me, and I have been arguing with Him that I should not do this. Only this evening a little while ago I got peace concerning the matter and have agreed to obey Him, and now I have come to tell you just some things that He has done for me."

He then called the conference to prayer. One participant said later, "I remember how the little company prostrated themselves on the mats on their faces . . . and then how for a long time, how long I do not know, man after man rose to his feet to pray, how there was such a confession of sin as most of us had never heard before, and such crying for mercy and help."[4]

May God send us men and women who will once again lay hold of Him in prayer until the Spirit falls, the windows of heaven open, and we can once more see a cloud the size of a man's hand.

CHAPTER 2

LEARNING FROM THE PSALMIST

Psalms 8, 51, 119, 139

When I come to God in prayer, he always looks to what the aim of my petition is. My comfort? My joy? Or that He be glorified. We need to learn that it is God's plan to bless me in order that I may be a blessing. Prayer is answered not to be consumed on self but to be passed on.

—Andrew Murray

Teach me, Lord, the meaning of Your statutes, and I will always keep them. Help me understand Your instruction, and I will obey it and follow it with all my heart.

—Psalm 119:33–34

OF ALL THE BOOKS of the Bible we turn to when we don't know what to pray, the Psalms would have to rank at the top. In the Psalms we read many of the prayers and songs of David. They resonate in our hearts. He says what we wish we had the ability to say. To pray the Psalms is one of the richest and most powerful experiences we can ever know in prayer. At the same time, we are praying the words of a "man after God's own heart" who struggled just as we struggle.

It is in prayer that we get a spiritual adjustment. I go to the chiropractor and massage therapist about once a month for my back. During those visits they check my spinal alignment, working out the spots where my back and body are resistant. Similarly when I pray, I am aligning myself with the purposes of God and identifying any areas of resistance.

Prayer is the most difficult part of the Christian life to me. It *should* be like breathing, but often it's like exercise. I find that prayer is sweet, but there are times when I seem to have no spiritual appetite for sweets. When I read books by the great men and women of prayer, I feel like a spiritual pigmy.

While we all acknowledge that we could do more praying than we're doing, we also know it is a discipline that must be developed. It's easier to read a book on prayer than to pray. It's easier to attend a prayer conference than to pray. I'm reminded of the words of Warren Wiersbe: "Lack of prayer does not handicap us; it paralyzes us."

It's easy to substitute a devotional book for prayer. But while a devotional book can prime the pump, it's no substitute for living water. John Bunyan wrote, "You can do more than pray after you have prayed, but you cannot do more than pray until you have prayed."

In this chapter I want us to look at several psalms and see what we can learn about prayer and praying from David and others. Whether written by someone famous or anonymous, it is obvious they were written by men whose hearts were stirred by God. Let's start by asking God to reveal Himself to us. If our prayers are going to be heard, we must allow God to search our hearts.

EVERYTHING WE ARE, EVERYTHING WE'RE NOT

In the Psalms we see prayers that address issues like suffering, fear, courage, confidence, doubt, attacks of the enemy, loneliness, and reputation. There is joy and gratitude in the Psalms. There is praise in the midst of pain. You find someone crying out for understanding at the beginning of a psalm, then rallying to deliver a declaration of hope by the end. There are few subjects off limits in these prayers. There is a depth of feeling in these words that all of us can identify with.

The psalmists often tell us they looked to Jehovah God in prayer, sometimes in song. Many of these prayers were used during worship in the temple after the second exile. I am sure that many who learned these songs also found themselves quoting them in their own prayers. When you read the Psalms, you find the writer often turning to prayer in the middle of the song. A sense of God's presence would overwhelm them, and they would turn to Him in praise or petition.

Psalm 8 takes the form of a prayer:

> LORD, our Lord, how magnificent is Your name
> throughout the earth! You have covered the
> heavens with Your majesty. Because of Your
> adversaries, You have established a strong-
> hold from the mouths of children and nursing
> infants, to silence the enemy and the avenger.
> When I observe Your heavens, the work of Your
> fingers, the moon and the stars, which You set
> in place, what is man that You remember him,
> the son of man that You look after him? You
> made him little less than God and crowned
> him with glory and honor. You made him lord
> over the works of Your hands; You put every-
> thing under his feet: all the sheep and oxen,
> as well as animals in the wild, birds of the sky,
> and fish of the sea passing through the currents
> of the seas. LORD, our Lord, how magnificent is
> Your name throughout the earth!

We should stand in awe at the thought that God even con-
siders or listens to us. What is man? He is God's only creature
that can pray and boldly approach His throne of grace. What is
man? He is a sinner in need of an advocate.

The opening and closing stanzas of Psalm 8 are addressed
to God. In this psalm we understand that even God has adver-
saries—people who oppose His name, work, and purpose in

this world, those who question His care and providence. I am reminded when I read this psalm of who I am and who God is.

C. S. Lewis said this psalm was "a short, exquisite lyric."[1] It is a reminder to us of the glory and majesty of God. It reminds me who I'm talking to when I pray. He's not my buddy, my pal, or the guy upstairs. He is the majestic Creator. David begins by calling Him "LORD, our Lord"—Jehovah Adonai. Creation cannot fully reveal such a God. Words are inadequate to describe such a God. This psalm reminds me I am just a man.

We have a place in the Smoky Mountains where I often retreat to study and think. It's where I am most inspired to write and prepare sermons. Often at night I find myself stepping out on the back porch and looking up into the sky to see the stars. There are no lights to hinder their beauty, and the moon seems clearer there. In the mornings I can look out and see Greenbrier Ridge, the longest ridge in those mountains, and see God's glory in their colors. No man-made structures block my view of this ridge created by God. I can hear Him rumbling through the hills and valleys as the storms approach. I can feel Him in the wind as it rushes down toward the valley. In that place I find myself saying, "What is man that you are mindful of Him?" It turns my heart to Jehovah Adonai.

WORD UP, DOWN, AND ALL AROUND

One thing I encourage people to do is to pray the Word. When in doubt, say what the people in the Bible said. You never go wrong praying the Scripture. Psalm 119 is an incredible passage about the Word of God. It was written as one of nine acrostic psalms so it could be memorized by all Hebrew children. Each of the twenty-two stanzas corresponds to the twenty-two letters of the Hebrew alphabet. To me it's a great passage to pray, reminding us of the important balance between the Word and prayer.

It is clear that the psalmist had determined in his heart to make the Word of God the governing principle in his life. He would not be governed by whims, political correctness, or the changing winds of the times. He was committed to staying anchored to the rock. I believe the Word was, in effect, the boundary for his praying, the place where he realigned his thinking.

Notice that God is mentioned in every verse. Every verse except verses 90, 122, and 132 have a reference to the Word of God. The psalmist refers to himself 325 times. It is a very personal psalm.

The different names for the Word contained in this psalm are significant. They teach us something about the character of God and His Word to us. Our prayers should be bathed in an understanding of God's Word. He has spoken and has not stuttered. When we understand that God is serious about His Word, then we know how to talk to Him.

- "Law" (*torah*) is used twenty-five times. It means "to direct, guide, or instruct." It is the summary word for all God has said. It goes far beyond what most people think, not limited to just the Ten Commandments. Ask God to direct you and guide you according to the Word as you pray.

- "Word" (*dabar*) is used twenty-four times. It comes from the verb meaning "to set forth in speech." It is God's revealed will. Ask God to make His will known to you as you pray.

- "Judgments" or "Ordinances" (*mispatim*) is used twenty-three times. It is from a verb meaning "to set upright, to govern, or to judge." God has given us a judicial ruling He expects us to heed. Ask God to keep you in line with His Word as you pray for others. It's not about your standards but His.

- "Testimonies" (*hedot*) is used twenty-three times. It is from a verb meaning "to bear witness." God's law bears witness of God's will and mind. Pray that your time alone with God will be a consistent testimony of your absolute dependence on Him. Don't just talk about prayer—pray!

- "Statutes" or "Decrees" (*huqqim*) is used twenty-one times. It means "to engrave or inscribe." Pray that God's Word will be engraved on your heart and mind. Read your Bible as a love letter from God to you.

- "Commandment" (*dath*) is used twenty-two times. It means "an order issued by an authority." God's Word is not His opinion. It is based on His authority to decree, command, and rule. As you pray, yield your thoughts, opinions, and plans to God.

- "Precepts" (*piqqudim*) is used twenty-one times. It means "to place in trust." God has entrusted His Word to man. We need to hear it, heed it, memorize it, study it, obey it, and meditate on it. As you pray, place your situation in

His trust. God has trusted you with His Word. Trust Him that He knows the best way to answer your prayer.

- "Saying," "Promises," or "Word" (*'imra*) is used nineteen times. It means "to bring to light." God's Word reveals. And what is revealed should be confessed. Ask God to bring to light any part of your heart that has grown dark. Ask Him to reveal any root of bitterness, stronghold, or area that is not surrendered to Him.

- "Way" is used thirteen times. It refers to "a road to be walked or a course of action to be taken that is marked out by God's law." Ask God as you rise from prayer that you will walk in a manner worthy of the gospel. Ask Him to empower you to remember His promises as you make decisions through the day.

The psalmist took these truths about the Truth and turned them into short, sentence prayers throughout Psalm 119, helping us clearly see that if we want a blessed life, our praying should conform to the Word of God. No matter how much we love God, we must be honest in seeking Him that we might live a life established, steady, and consistent with His statutes. You will often hear the psalmist asking that he might "keep," "walk," "obey," and "learn" the Word. He saw a connection between the Word and prayer, between talk and walk. Here are a few examples of His prayers within this powerful chapter:

> If only my ways were committed to keeping
> Your statutes! (v. 5)

Open my eyes so that I may see wonderful
things in Your law. (v. 18)

Help me understand Your instruction, and
I will obey it and follow it with all my heart.
Help me stay on the path of Your commands,
for I take pleasure in it. Turn my heart to Your
decrees and not to material gain. Turn my eyes
from looking at what is worthless; give me life
in Your ways. Confirm what You said to Your
servant, for it produces reverence for You.
(vv. 34–38)

Before I was afflicted I went astray, but now
I keep Your word. You are good and You do what
is good; teach me Your statutes. (vv. 67–68)

How I love Your teaching! It is my meditation
all day long. (v. 97)

Sustain me as You promised, and I will live; do
not let me be ashamed of my hope. (v. 116)

These verses were written as praise to God for His Word.
But as the psalmist wrote, he often turned to prayer because
God had touched his life through the Word. He prayed that
God would give him insight and understanding, asking for guid-
ance as he studied God's revealed wisdom. And in so doing,

he teaches us much about prayer as he teaches us much about God's Word.

GETTING PERSONAL

David knew God well enough to know that he needed His empowerment if he was ever to make the needed adjustments in his life, if he was ever to become what God had called him to be. One of his most personal prayers is captured in Psalm 139, "Search me, God, and know my heart; test me and know my concerns. See if there is any offensive way in me; lead me in the everlasting way" (vv. 23–24).

When God searches, He does a thorough search. He doesn't just casually look; He digs deep. When I travel to Israel, it's not hard to see they are serious about national security. In America, all we have to do is take off our shoes. (I'm still not sure why we do that.) But in Israel, soldiers work security at the airport. They look you in the eyes and watch your body language. They make you go through your own bag while they watch. They are trained to read people, and they take their job seriously.

We tend to hope that God will not run us through a security screening. We hope He will not take seriously the psalmist's prayer to search us, try us, examine us, and show us anything that stands in the way. Hurtful things like laziness, apathy, indifference, hypocrisy, fear, and even pride are things that God will readily point out if we pray like this.

David was asking God to evaluate his life, his heart, and his mind. In fact, Psalm 139 begins with the statement, "Lord, You have searched me and known me." It is a declaration that

God knows all things, even all things about *us*. But rather than feeling intruded upon, David prayed for God to search Him. He asked God to investigate his conduct and examine his heart. The last thing he wanted was to be self-deluded about where he was with his Lord. Look at what David prayed:

- "Know"—Know my heart and my thoughts. Search me thoroughly. Get beyond the surface to what I think about, to my values, goals, and purposes, to what occupies my imagination and controls my will.
- "Test"—David's desire was to be tested in heart and mind and proved faithful.
- "See"—What David was asking God to look for in him— any kind of hurtful or "offensive way"—can also be translated "wicked way," "way of pain," "way of grief," "way of iniquity," or "way of falsehood." These are ways that lead to grief and would ultimately lead to chastisement or discipline or bitter repentance. We need to ask God to see if there is any tendency in us to forsake Him, to substitute anything or anyone else for Him, or to drift away from true worship.
- "Lead me"—To be led in the "everlasting way" can be translated "the way that leads to everlasting life" or "the way of righteousness." This reflects a hunger and thirst for being in right relationship with God.

We can also look to the psalmist as a guide to prayer when we have fallen short of God's standards. "It is time for the LORD to act, for they have broken Your law" (119:126). Why is it time for God to act? Because the people have broken His law.

> The earth is polluted by its inhabitants, for they have transgressed teachings, overstepped decrees, and broken the everlasting covenant. (Isa. 24:5)

> For the hearers of the law are not righteous before God, but the doers of the law will be declared righteous. (Rom. 2:13)

> Anyone who turns his ear away from hearing the law—even his prayer is detestable. (Prov. 28:9)

We live in an age where our children and grandchildren are being taught that there are no absolutes, that everything is relative. It's time for God's people to pray that there will be a return to truth. It is imperative that we pray the enemy doesn't get a foothold in the minds of the next generation.

This brings me to Psalm 85:6, "Will You not revive us again so that Your people may rejoice in You?" This is a watershed verse—a heartfelt prayer for revival and renewal. We have tried everything but God. Is it not time for us to seek Him that we may have revival?

THE PEACE OF BELIEVING

I was visiting with a fellow pastor one day. He knew my heart for revival and awakening. He also knew that a church was "looking at me" as a possible pastor. I wasn't interested in making a move, but I asked him what he thought about the possibility. He said, "Catt, they don't need any of that revival stuff. That worked in the 1970s, but that won't work anymore. They need a pastor with a cutting-edge approach. The days of Bible conferences and prayer conferences are over." I thought to myself, "And that is exactly why the church lacks power today."

Paul, writing to the Romans, prayed, "May the God of hope fill you with all joy and peace in believing, so that you may overflow with hope by the power of the Holy Spirit" (15:13). When Donald Grey Barnhouse was on the radio in the early twentieth century, he did six studies on this one verse. He said:

> This verse is a great summary of the blessed life in the brotherhood formed by our oneness in Jesus Christ. The source of that life is the God of hope. The measure of that life is that we shall be filled "with all joy and peace." The quality of that life is joy and peace which He desires for us. The condition of that life is faith—we enter it by believing. The purpose of that life is that we might abound. The enabling of that life is divine power. The director of that life is the Holy Spirit.[2]

As I write this chapter, we are in the middle of an economic meltdown in America. Wall Street is taking a hit on a daily basis. Oil is overpriced. Houses are being repossessed. Banks and mortgage companies are being bailed out by the government. It is a reminder to me that God often works in times of crisis to set His people to praying. He can use bad news to take us to the good news for answers and hope.

Paul did not write these words sitting in a luxury condo on the French Riviera. He wrote most of his letters from prison. He wrote during a time of increasing persecution and growing heresy. Yet he prayed that they might have joy and peace in believing and abound in hope. If they could do it under Roman oppression, why can't we? The world and its system lack answers, but *we* have the answer. Revival will bring joy to joyless people, peace in the midst of stressful times, and hope in the midst of a hopeless situation.

Isn't this what the psalmist did over and over? He brought God into his desperate situations. He remembered the Word. He remembered the Lord. He remembered the promises, and his cries turned to praise, his despair to hope.

IF IT'S BIG ENOUGH TO WORRY ABOUT, IT'S BIG ENOUGH TO PRAY ABOUT.

Our God is the source of our hope. Not Wall Street. Not the government. When there is an issue, big or small, we should turn to God in prayer. Nothing is too big or too little for our God. If it's big enough to worry about, it's big enough to pray about. It seems from reading the Psalms, there was nothing that the psalmist wouldn't pray about. When you consider that David was the author of many of the Psalms, maybe it was his prayer life that caused him to be called "a man after God's own heart."

HOW BAD DO WE WANT IT?

When I was serving as a youth minister in Oklahoma in the 1970s, I had a young man in my youth group named Ray Sanders. Ray came from a broken home and grew up in a tough situation, but he became one of my favorite students of all time. Even today, Ray has a smile, a joy, and a faith like few men I know. To see how God is using him is a blessing to my heart. I asked him to share a story with me that reveals how God can work through prayer to fill us with joy and peace in believing:

> A few years ago my wife and I sat down for dinner with our children at a local restaurant. While we were waiting on our meal, my wife noticed the diamond in her wedding ring was missing. She was devastated! Panic was written all over her face. Tears began to appear.
>
> We searched every inch on and under the table. She combed the restaurant like a CSI detective. Nothing. She rushed outside, turning the car inside out. Nothing. We had arrived at the restaurant in separate vehicles, coming from two different places. In desperation she decided to return to a large retailer she had just visited before we'd met at the restaurant.

I tried appealing to her logic, but she was undeterred. She left about the time our meal arrived. As the kids and I bowed our heads, we prayed for my wife to find her diamond. It was already dark outside, and the retailer would be closing within the hour. Time and circumstances were not on her side. Besides, she wasn't sure if she lost the diamond the same day or earlier. It was hopeless in my opinion.

As we left the restaurant, I walked into the darkness of the evening with one of my kids in tow. As I stepped off the curb, my son stepped the opposite direction. We bumped each other, stumbling on the black asphalt parking lot. As I struggled to regain my balance, a tiny sparkle caught my attention by the light of the moon. My first reaction was to ignore the remote possibility that it might have been the answer to my prayer. I paused, took a deep breath, and knelt down to investigate further. There was no mistaking what I had discovered. It became very clear in a matter of seconds that despite unimaginable odds, despite a sea of darkness, and despite my lack of faith, the diamond my wife was searching for had been recovered!

My children were startled when I jumped to my feet and screamed, "It's a miracle!" Others in the parking lot must have thought I'd lost my mind. "Daddy, God answered our prayers," were the words from my little one. "He sure did, baby, He sure did," I replied.

As we entered the retailer where my wife was desperately searching for a needle in a hay-stack, we found her surrounded by a group of employees committed to the hunt. I swore the children to secrecy as I made my way toward her. As I approached her, tears still in her eyes, I asked her a simple question: "Did it mean a lot to you when I gave it to you the first time?" The painful expression on her face required no reply. "Then I hope it means as much to you now," I said, as I placed the diamond in her hand.

Cheers accompanied my announcement. Disbelief melted among God's provision. Our growing little family experienced God in a way that can only be described as miraculous.

When life gets desperate, things look hope-less, and I wonder if anyone really cares, I think back to that dark night when God delivered our miracle. The One who placed the twinkle in the stars returned the sparkle to my life. Matthew was right—"With man this is impos-sible, but with God all things are possible." He has and continues to do it, time and time again.

When's the last time you went before God with that kind of desperation and intensity? When's the last time you believed God for a miracle, for something you couldn't explain or take credit for? Too often we look for a pass from problems rather than seeing our problems as an opportunity to trust God.

SORRY SINNERS

We also find prayers for repentance in the Psalms—none more personal than the prayer of repentance in Psalm 51. David laid it all on the line. His sin and failure became a song and a prayer. These words remind us how we should pray when we fall into sin.

> Be gracious to me, God, according to Your faithful love; according to Your abundant compassion, blot out my rebellion. Wash away my guilt, and cleanse me from my sin. For I am conscious of my rebellion, and my sin is always before me. Against You—You alone—I have sinned and done this evil in Your sight. So You are right when You pass sentence; You are blameless when You judge. Indeed, I was guilty when I was born; I was sinful when my mother conceived me.
>
> Surely You desire integrity in the inner self, and You teach me wisdom deep within. Purify me with hyssop, and I will be clean; wash me, and I will be whiter than snow. Let me hear joy

and gladness; let the bones You have crushed rejoice. Turn Your face away from my sins and blot out all my guilt.

God, create a clean heart for me and renew a steadfast spirit within me. Do not banish me from Your presence or take Your Holy Spirit from me. Restore the joy of Your salvation to me, and give me a willing spirit. Then I will teach the rebellious Your ways, and sinners will return to You.

Save me from the guilt of bloodshed, God, the God of my salvation, and my tongue will sing of Your righteousness. Lord, open my lips, and my mouth will declare Your praise. You do not want a sacrifice, or I would give it; You are not pleased with a burnt offering. The sacrifice pleasing to God is a broken spirit. God, You will not despise a broken and humbled heart. (vv. 1–16)

There is no Watergate cover-up here. It's all out in the open. God expects and respects honesty. There is no whitewashing when it comes to our sin and guilt. Like David, we must come clean if we want our prayers to be heard. No self-justification, no finger pointing. This is our model—an honest prayer of a repentant man before a holy God. This is not just a private confession of David's guilt; it is a public expression of repentance and a longing for restoration.

David had a broken heart. He had sinned against God, and he cried out for mercy, pardon, grace, cleansing, and restoration. He didn't make excuses but got right to the point. This is a personal prayer from a man who had sinned, yes, but who deeply, genuinely longed for restoration of fellowship.

Conviction that doesn't lead to confession is shallow. It may be remorse, but it's not repentance. David had violated God's law. He had perverted God's moral standard and missed the mark. This prayer is the classic example in all of Scripture of the difference between feeling sorry over the consequences of getting caught and sorrow because of the sin itself. David knew his sins were deeper than adultery and attempted murder. His sin was first and foremost against God Himself.

We blame the times in which we live, the temptations around us, the tendencies we've inherited, and the poor training we've received, but we too rarely look in our own mirror and see the sinner in it. David used the personal pronouns "I," "my," "me," or "mine" at least thirty-five times. He pled with God to pardon him, purify him, and restore power to his life. When he prayed, "God, create a clean heart for me," the word "create" is the same word used in Genesis 1, speaking of the creation of the world. It is something only God can do. We can say man creates, but actually he only discovers what God has already put there. David is asking for nothing less than a miraculous transformation—create what is not there and renew what *is* there because it's in a wrecked condition right now.

When God remakes us, He doesn't just patch us up and send us on our way. We don't need tune-ups; we need overhauls.

David wanted a new heart. He didn't want the Spirit to forsake him like He had with Saul. David knew, even though he'd forgotten for a season, that he could not survive without the Lord. Only the Holy Spirit can give us a steadfast spirit and a willing spirit.

Andrew Murray wrote, "When I come to God in prayer, He always looks to what the aim is of my petition. My comfort? My joy? Or that He be glorified. We need to learn that it is God's plan to bless me in order that I may be a blessing. Prayer is answered not to be consumed on self but to be passed on."

David understood the bigger picture in his big confession. He knew that ministry could come out of this failure. He wanted to be restored so he could teach and reach others.

"Restore the joy of Your salvation to me, and give me a willing spirit." Sin causes us to lose our joy—a joy we

> **JOY IS WHAT YOU LOSE WHEN YOU SIN AND WHAT YOU HAVE WHEN YOU'RE WALKING WITH GOD.**

won't get back just by going to hear a preacher who can fire us up. We won't find it restored by exercise and a self-help program. Joy only comes through repentance and confession. Joy is what you lose when you sin and what you have when you're walking with God. The presence of joy is hard to define, but its absence is easy to detect.

When you read all the things David asked for in verses 7–12, you realize that he recognized all he had lost when he was living in sin. The longer we live, the easier it is to grow indifferent, cynical, and deaf to the still, small voice. We can become blind to our blind spots. As a pastor, I've watched people experience a revolutionary change in their lives when they finally became desperate and began to seek the Lord. I've seen marriages restored, prodigals return, and once carnal, self-centered men become godly leaders in their homes. I've seen homosexuals delivered from their bondage. I've seen drug addicts and alcoholics set free. I can say emphatically that it hasn't happened in a healing meeting or a "Let's all get happy and jump pews" meeting. It has happened in prayer meetings.

I can look at the answered prayers that have come from our intercessory prayer ministry and say that God is more willing to work than many of us are to pray. We've seen countless answers to prayers. Many were situations where folks had despaired of hope, but God came through at their lowest point. When sin was so dark and hope was lost, God showed up!

Since the release of *Fireproof*, we've heard from people all across the country whose lives have been dramatically changed by the film. Men have been freed from the chains of pornography, marriages have been restored, and some have even accepted the free gift of salvation while sitting in their seats at the theater! Here's an example of one such story we received on our Web site:

> My wife of thirteen years handed me divorce papers on the Monday evening before the movie came out. The script for the movie could have been written about us. We are both good people, but we were not being good to each

other. I got a call from a friend on Saturday, insisting that my wife and I go see this movie. I was afraid to even ask her, but I did. We went to the afternoon movie on Sunday. Wow—it was us on the screen.

We went home and talked about a lot of things, and both of us said we were sorry. We decided to stay together, to start going to church together again, and to treat each other the way we should have been all along.

My wife called her lawyer on Monday and told him that she didn't want a divorce, and I did the same. We ordered *The Love Dare* for both of us on Tuesday and the marriage kit as well. Thank you so much for showing us that we aren't the only couple with the problems that these people had and for giving us a new direction to go in. I love my wife and am look-ing forward to our new life together!

When prisoners go to God, He sets captives free. When we sin, we have an advocate (see 1 John 1:6–2:2). As my friend Ron Dunn used to say, "Our advocate is related to the Judge, and He's never lost a case." Why spend time trying to justify or excuse anything that is against the will and Word of God? Go to God. Plead your case. Trust your Advocate. The Judge of heaven can and will rule "not guilty" to all who come to the mercy seat.

William Gurnall, a Puritan preacher, said, "When people do not mind what God speaks to them in His Word, God doesn't mind what they say to Him in prayer." I think the psalmist would agree.

CHAPTER 3

THE PRAYER OF THE PENITENT

Psalm 32

Prayer will make a man cease from sin, or sin will entice a man to cease from prayer.
—**John Bunyan**

Be gracious to me, God, according to Your faithful love; according to Your abundant compassion, blot out my rebellion.... Against You—You alone—I have sinned and done this evil in Your sight. So You are right when You pass sentence; You are blameless when You judge.
—**Psalm 51:1, 4**

IN THE THIRD Indiana Jones movie, *Indiana Jones and the Last Crusade*, Indy and his father are on a search to find the holy grail before the Nazis beat them to it. When they finally do locate the grail's resting place, they must first pass three word puzzles before they can ultimately reach it. The first clue is, "Only the penitent man shall pass!" Just in time, Indiana Jones concludes that the penitent man comes to God on his knees. So by stooping down, Indy misses being killed by the trap set for him. He passes the first test: the penitent man kneels before God.

Some of the hardest words to say in the English language are "I have sinned." None of us like to say it. It's always easier to point blame at others, but until this point is driven home in our hearts, we cannot have the kind of prayer life God intends.

The two most costly things on earth are not diamonds or gold. The two most costly things on earth are salvation and sin. Salvation cost God's Son His life to pay the price for our sin. To have fellowship with God, we must confess that which breaks our fellowship. Sin is a costly price to pay.

While visiting Scotland in 2000, I spent some time with Colin Peckham. Colin and his wife, Mary, have been used mightily of God to speak about revival, prayer, and the Spirit-filled life. Colin took us on a tour of Edinburgh. As we were walking around, we went into a church, and a small stool caught my eye.

I asked Colin the meaning of the stool. He said in the old days when people were caught in sin, they would have to sit on the mourner's stool during the church service until the preacher was convinced they had repented of sin and forsaken it. I asked if it was used any longer. With a sad look on his face Colin replied, "In this place? Not in a long, long time."

Then it hit me. I preach in churches all across the country, and I have found a consistent problem. There is little joy on people's faces. They sit, soak, and sour. It doesn't seem to matter if they're part of a liturgical church or a church on the cutting edge, they all seem to display a lack of joy. They sit with arms folded, looking like they just drank a fifth of vinegar. What's the problem? They are concealing their transgressions. You can never be a worshipper until you're a confessor. There has to be a humbling before there is a hallelujah. There has to be cleansing before there can be shouting.

DESPERATE COVER-UPS

It's easy to conceal sin. It's natural to try covering up our shortcomings. Once when I was a kid, I had a sparkler left over from the Fourth of July, and I brilliantly decided to light it and twirl it around the house. By the grace of God, I didn't light it on the carpet. But in my stupidity, I lit it in the kitchen, where my parents had just put down a new linoleum floor. It didn't take me long to realize this was not a good decision.

Immediately I began trying to cover up my crime. I scrubbed the floor with a sponge, but that did nothing to mask the numerous small holes the sparks had made in the floor. I used my model car paint to try to fill in the holes, but that didn't work either.

Only after exhausting all efforts to conceal my sin did I call my mom at work and tell her what I had done. It was dumb to do it in the first place, and even dumber to try to conceal it. After all, everyone knows that moms and God are all-knowing.

Adam and Eve tried to conceal their sin from God. Remember, they bought the lie of the serpent and then tried to hide by covering themselves and making excuses. Eve blamed the serpent, and Adam was dumb enough to blame God ("the woman You gave to be with me," Gen. 3:12). It cost them the garden of paradise and perfect fellowship with God.

Then there was Cain. The apple doesn't fall far from the tree, does it? Cain hadn't wanted to do things God's way. He'd brought an unacceptable sacrifice to the Lord, while his brother Abel had brought an acceptable one. And in his anger over this, Cain murdered his brother. Sin controlled him in that moment. The first family had (as far as we know) the first funeral. One son of Adam and Eve was dead; the other was a murderer.

But Cain not only committed murder; he also lied to God. He tried to cover it up. He denied knowing where his brother was. "Am I my brother's keeper?" he was famously quoted as saying (Gen. 4:9 NKJV). The apostle John would later write to remind us, "If we say, 'We have fellowship with Him,' and walk in darkness, we are lying and are not practicing the truth" (1 John 1:6). Cain seemingly came to bring a sacrifice in order to maintain fellowship with God, but he ended up being an angry liar and a murderer.

Achan is another person who tried to conceal his sin. God had given Joshua and the people clear instructions about what to do when they took Jericho. Everything was to be destroyed, none of it kept as personal plunder. "If you take any of those things, you will set apart the camp of Israel for destruction and bring disaster on it. For all the silver and gold, and the articles of bronze and iron, are dedicated to the LORD and must go into the LORD's treasury" (Josh. 6:18–19).

As this story continues to unfold, we read, "The Israelites, however, were unfaithful regarding the things set apart for destruction. Achan . . . took some of what was set apart, and the LORD's anger burned against the Israelites" (7:1). Achan was guilty of coveting, theft, and deception. He took what was to be set aside for the Lord. The result was that he and his family were stoned to death. Let's just say that Achan did not prosper by stealing and concealing.

A New Testament parallel would be Ananias and Sapphira. In the early days of the church when the Spirit was moving, they were guilty of trying to impress their peers. They sold a piece of land and pretended to give all of the proceeds from the sale to the church. They lied to God, to the church, and to the apostles. God struck both of them dead. God takes sin seriously.

Solomon wrote, "The one who conceals his sins will not prosper, but whoever confesses and renounces them will find mercy" (Prov. 28:13). The word "conceals" in this verse means to cover up with clothing, to hide. And the thing being hidden is our transgression—our sin against God and against others, areas where we have revolted and rebelled against authority.

Proverbs is clear: those who try to take this path "will not prosper." They will not move forward. Their lives will not be profitable. Spiritually, they will be off in a ditch.

FINGER POINTING

All the aforementioned Bible characters had one thing in common: they each tried to conceal their sin. But probably the most famous cover-up in Scripture is that of David. David was a great sinner, no doubt about it. But as we will see, he was an even greater repenter.

You know the story. David was supposed to be off at war, but he was lazy and stayed home. As a result he saw Bathsheba bathing, lusted after her, and took her for himself. Then to cover up his adultery, David plotted the murder of Bathsheba's husband.

For one year David did all he could to hide his sin. It would seem likely that he threatened his servants with certain death if they told anyone about that night. Finally the prophet Nathan approached the king and confronted him.

> The LORD sent Nathan to David. When he arrived, he said to him: "There were two men in a certain city, one rich and the other poor. The rich man had a large number of sheep and cattle, but the poor man had nothing except one small ewe lamb that he had bought. It lived and grew up with him and his children. It shared his meager food and drank from his cup; it slept in his arms, and it was like a daughter to him. Now a traveler came to the rich man, but the rich man could not bring himself to take one of his own sheep or cattle to prepare for the traveler who had come to him. Instead, he

took the poor man's lamb and prepared it for his guest." David was infuriated with the man and said to Nathan: "As surely as the LORD lives, the man who did this deserves to die! Because he has done this thing and shown no pity, he must pay four lambs for that lamb."

Nathan replied to David, "You are the man! This is what the LORD God of Israel says: 'I anointed you king over Israel, and I delivered you from the hand of Saul. I gave your master's house to you and your master's wives into your arms, and I gave you the house of Israel and Judah, and if that was not enough, I would have given you even more. Why then have you despised the command of the LORD by doing what I consider evil? You struck down Uriah the Hittite with the sword and took his wife as your own wife—you murdered him with the Ammorite's sword. Now therefore, the sword will never leave your house because you despised Me and took the wife of Uriah the Hittite to be your own wife."

This is what the LORD says, "I am going to bring disaster on you from your own family: I will take your wives and give them to another before your very eyes, and he will sleep with them publicly. You acted in secret, but I will do this before all Israel and in broad daylight."

David responded to Nathan, "I have sinned against the LORD." Then Nathan replied to David, "The LORD has taken away your sin; you will not die." (2 Sam. 12:1–13)

David was guilty of adultery and murder—the second sin an attempt to cover up the first. He may have tried to convince himself that he had gotten away with it or that it was justifiable, but Nathan had a word from God. "You are the man!"

COMING CLEAN

I believe one of the reasons David was spared from death and total devastation was because of his response. He didn't try to defend himself. He didn't make excuses. He didn't go on Oprah or Dr. Phil and try to convince them it was a mistake. He didn't say, "It's my life, and what I do is my business," or "I've prayed, and I have a peace about it." What David had done was evil. He had sinned against the Lord. But David responded correctly to the prophet, and his life was spared.

Maybe God has sent someone into your life to speak the truth in love. How have you responded to them? Have you thrown up your defenses, or have you fallen to your knees? It takes a godly person with pure motives to stand up and serve as God's warning signal to other believers. To ignore them can bring disastrous results.

David was ready to repent. He knew he was going nowhere fast unless he came clean before the Lord and admitted the error of his ways. Psalm 32 is one of seven penitent psalms, the first of thirteen *maskil* psalms. The word *maskil* means to instruct. David wrote this psalm of personal confession for our instruction. His prayer reads like this:

How happy is the one whose transgression is forgiven, whose sin is covered! How happy is the man the LORD does not charge with sin, and in whose spirit is no deceit!

When I kept silent, my bones became brittle from my groaning all day long. For day and night Your hand was heavy on me; my strength was drained as in the summer's heat. *Selah.* Then I acknowledged my sin to You and did not conceal my iniquity. I said, "I will confess my transgressions to the LORD," and You took away the guilt of my sin. *Selah.*

Therefore let everyone who is faithful pray to You at a time that You may be found. When great floodwaters come, they will not reach him. You are my hiding place; You protect me from trouble. You surround me with joyful shouts of deliverance. *Selah.*

I will instruct you and show you the way to go; with My eye on you, I will give counsel. Do not be like a horse or mule, without

ONE OF THE REASONS DAVID WAS SPARED FROM DEATH AND TOTAL DEVASTATION WAS BECAUSE OF HIS RESPONSE.

understanding, that must be controlled with bit and bridle, or else it will not come near you.

Many pains come to the wicked, but the one who trusts in the LORD will have faithful love surrounding him. Be glad in the LORD and rejoice, you righteous ones; shout for joy, all you upright in heart.

In the first two verses, David described the evil he was confessing as "transgression," "sin," and "deceit." No beating around the bush or pointing fingers at someone else. Just gut-wrenching honesty before God. But notice he says there is forgiveness for transgression. God rolls away the burden. For sin there is a covering, and for deceit there is a cancelled debt. The sin debt has been paid. It was no longer reckoned to David's account.

David was no longer willing to conceal his sin. He was not interested in trying to deceive anyone. It was time to come clean before God—to acknowledge his sin, not to excuse it. He confessed his iniquity. He didn't try to hide it any longer. And the end result was restored communion. His life would no longer be marked by hypocrisy and duplicity.

David was now ready to worship. Why? Because he had turned to God in prayer and confessed his sin. He found that God forgave not only the sin but also the guilt of his sin. He then wrote the word "Selah," meaning to pause and think about what had just been said. God's grace should cause us to stop and reflect. His grace is greater than all our sin.

THE GREAT COMEBACK

In Psalm 51, David's prayer of repentance, he didn't wear a mask or strut with pride. The great king was no longer covering up or worried about what others might think. His one and only goal was to get back in right fellowship with the living God.

We looked at this psalm in the previous chapter, but remember again some of the touching, passionate words and phrases: how he admitted, "Against You—You alone—I have sinned and done this evil in Your sight"; how he pled, "Let me hear joy and gladness; let the bones You have crushed rejoice"; how he recognized the humble path back to restoration and wholeness, "You do not want a sacrifice, or I would give it; You are not pleased with a burnt offering. The sacrifice pleasing to God is a broken spirit. God, You will not despise a broken and humbled heart."

More than anything, David wanted again the joy, favor, and fellowship he had once experienced with the Lord. He remembered the times when fellowship with God was sweet. He remembered the times when he danced before the Lord as the ark of the covenant was brought to Jerusalem. He was willing to do whatever it took to be back in right relationship with God. He was looking for unblemished, untarnished intimacy with the Almighty.

So he openly confessed his sin and asked God to purify him. David mentioned "hyssop," the Hebrew herb used in ceremonial cleansing of lepers. He was asking God to "un-sin" him. He wanted to be clean to the core. No soft scrubbing, whitewashing, or quick fix would do. David wanted God to wash him—

a chore that in David's day was done by pounding clothes against rocks or stomping on them until they were clean.

David pointed out at least nine areas of his life affected by his sin: his eyes (v. 3), his mind or inner self (v. 6), his ears (v. 8), his bones (v. 8), his heart (v. 10), his peace (v. 10), his joy (v. 12), his spirit (v. 12), his gifts and talents (v. 15).

David was utterly miserable in his sin. His joy was gone. His peace was gone. His body ached all over. There had been consequences to that one night of fleeting pleasure, and he wanted to get back to the way it had been before.

From this purifying came great joy. There is no joy when sin is present. Think of all the broken lives and hardened hearts in this world because of sin. Saul's sin was pride. Samson's sin was lust. Judas's sin was coveting. Millions have lost their joy and peace because of these three sins.

But our God is willing to hear the prayers of sinners. Micah wrote, "Who is a God like You, removing iniquity and passing over rebellion for the remnant of His inheritance? He does not hold on to His anger forever, because He delights in faithful love. He will again have compassion on us; He will vanquish our iniquities. You will cast all our sins into the depths of the sea. You will show loyalty to Jacob and faithful love to Abraham, as You swore to our fathers from days long ago" (7:18–20).

Of all the gods worshipped in this world, of all the idols given allegiance, none is like our God. He is willing to forgive sin and show mercy. He pardons. He demonstrates compassion. He casts our sins into a sea of forgetfulness and remembers them no more.

My youth minister growing up was James Miller—the only youth minister I had in those critical years. The youth program in our church didn't have a budget. Our youth group never went to camp. But James taught me something about the love of God through his work, his testimony, and his lifestyle. Even today at age seventy he is still serving the Lord, despite a life that has been filled with heartbreak.

James had three children. But before they were very old, their mother left with another man, leaving James to basically raise his three kids by himself. One of these, his daughter Nell, had a baby boy out of wedlock, adding to his family's troubles. A few years ago, in fact, she died tragically. But before she died, she wrote James a letter. He shared it with me, and I thought it was appropriate for this chapter.

> Hi Dad,
>
> It's me. I have so much to say that I don't know where to start. My son has made me realize what a wonderful father you are. Of course, I always knew you were great! But now I realize how truly great you are.
>
> I have so many questions. One, how did you ever do it? How did you financially, emotionally, physically, and mentally raise three kids alone? Two, how did you teach us to respect and honor you without tanning our hides every time we did wrong? Three, how do you know when to hold onto them and when to let them

fall down and when to let them go to learn lessons on their own?

My son is wonderful. I know he wasn't conceived the way God tells us children should be. Believe it or not, it took twenty-six years and my son to make me realize why God gave us the rules He has. I always thought they were set up to keep us from having fun or to limit us. But now I realize they are in place to make life easier, to make it more enjoyable. Thank you, Dad, for being the best father and granddad anyone could ask for. You are my hero.

I love you always,

Nell

David closed Psalm 51 with a promise that still rings true to this day: "The sacrifice pleasing to God is a broken spirit. God, You will not despise a broken and humbled heart" (v. 17). It's never too late to come home. God is not reluctant or unwilling to welcome you back. Remember the story of the prodigal son? His father lavishly celebrated his homecoming and embraced him with arms of unconditional love. How much more does your heavenly Father love you and want you home?

"Therefore repent and turn back, that your sins may be wiped out so that seasons of refreshing may come from the presence of the Lord" (Acts 3:19).

CHAPTER 4

LORD, TEACH US TO PRAY

Luke 11

The act of praying is the very highest energy of which the human mind is capable; praying, that is, with the total concentration of the faculties.
—Samuel Taylor Coleridge

He was praying in a certain place, and when He finished, one of His disciples said to Him, "Lord, teach us to pray, just as John also taught his disciples."
—Luke 11:1

BLAISE PASCAL ONCE WROTE, "There are three kinds of people: those who have sought God and found him, and these are reasonable and happy; those who seek God and have not yet found him, and these are reasonable and unhappy; and those who neither seek God nor find him, and these are unreasonable and unhappy."[1] Seeking God in prayer is simply foundational to the kind of life we all want. The family, the home, the church, and the nation will rise and fall on the basis of our prayers.

If we are going to leave a legacy of faith, we must teach our children to pray. If we are going to see power in our churches, we must have men of prayer in the pulpits. If we are going to reach the next generation for Christ, fulfill the Great Commission, and change our culture in the process, we must be people who have learned to get hold of God. O. Hallesby wrote:

> Our family has been a believing and praying family for three generations. The elders have prayed faithfully for their descendants. During my whole life I have walked in the prayers of my parents and in answer to these prayers. I reap, in truth, what others have sown. My friend, if you are not able to leave your children a legacy in the form of money or goods, do not worry about that. And do not wear yourself to death either physically or spiritually in order to accumulate a great deal of property for your children; but see to it, night and day, that you pray for them. Then you will leave them

a great legacy of answers to prayer, which will
follow them all the days of their life. Then you
may calmly and with good conscience depart
from them.[2]

A few years ago, U.S. News & World Report ran a cover
story entitled "The Power of Prayer." I am always interested to
see how the world views prayer, as opposed to how we as believers view this vital aspect of our faith. According to the article,
"a recent Roper poll found that nearly half of all Americans said
they pray or meditate every day—far more than those who reg-
ularly participate in religious services. . . . Prayer has been called
the 'native language' of the soul—the universal expression of
an innate human desire to make contact with the divine."

In addition the magazine conducted a poll to determine
how, when, and why people pray. Here are a few facts from
nearly six thousand responses:

- 75.6% say they are Christians.
- 64% say they pray more than once a day.
- 56% say they pray most often for family members.
- 3.3% say they pray for strangers.
- 38.3% say that the most important purpose of prayer is
  intimacy with God.
- 41.2% say their prayers are often answered.
- 1.5% say their prayers are never answered.
- 73.9% say when their prayers are not answered, the most
  important reason is that they did not fit into God's plan.

- 5.1% say they pray most often in a house of worship.
- 79.4% say they pray most often at home.[3]

I'm not sure what a poll like this reveals. After all, there are millions of so-called evangelicals in America, and this is just a small sampling. But I know that few of our seminaries have any classes teaching the next generation of church leaders about prayer. I went through a Baptist school and seminary without having even one class on prayer. Whatever I have learned about prayer has been from the Scriptures, from men and women of prayer, and from quality books on the subject. Andrew Murray wrote something that has convicted my heart as a minister:

> The enemy will use all his power to lead the Christian, and above all the minister, to neglect prayer. He knows that however admirable the sermon may be, however attractive the service, however faithful the pastoral visitation, none of these things can damage him or his kingdom if prayer is neglected. When the Church shuts herself up to the power of the inner chamber, and the soldiers of the Lord have received on their knees 'power from on high,' then the powers of darkness will be shaken and souls will be delivered. In the Church, on the mission field, with the minister and his congregation, everything depends on the faithful exercise of the power of prayer.[4]

I recall Vance Havner telling me about the Southern Baptist Convention in Los Angeles in 1981. The event organizers had asked an elderly Miss Bertha Smith, famous Southern Baptist missionary to China and a long-recognized prayer warrior, to lead the group in prayer. Havner said, "She told God things about Southern Baptists that Southern Baptists didn't want God to know!"

O Lord, teach us to pray.

Prayer is too often our last resort, not our first option. We tack on prayers and ask God to bless our planned-out, prearranged events in church. We plan our lives and activities and then ask God to bless our efforts. I heard of a church that was going through a difficult season. The hallways were filled with tension, and the business meetings were just short of an all-out war. One man stood up in the business meeting and said, "Brethren, I think we should go to God in prayer."

ARE WE MERELY ASKING FOR THINGS WE WANT, OR ARE WE YIELDING OURSELVES TO WHAT GOD WANTS?

One lady said from the back, "Oh, no! Has it come to that?"

Even though nothing is more important in the Christian life than prayer, I often wonder how much praying we really do. And when we do pray, are we praying biblically, or are we just worrying on our knees? Are we just asking for things we want, or are we yielding ourselves to what God wants for our lives? Would we know an answered prayer if we saw one?

My friend Charles Lowery, a motivational speaker and psychologist, as well as a former pastor, tells the story of a man who was lost in the woods and couldn't find his way out. Finally the man got down on his knees and prayed, "God, I'm lost! I'm going to die! Please help me get out of these woods!" When someone later asked him, "Did God answer your prayer?" the man responded, "No, He didn't have time. Just after I got off my knees, some guy appeared from nowhere and led me out."

I've heard it said that God answers prayers one of four ways: 1) "Yes," 2) "No," 3) "Later," or 4) "You've got to be kidding Me!" God hears and God answers, but often it may not be in line with what we want Him to do. As a Garth Brooks song from the early 1990s says it, "Some of God's greatest gifts are unanswered prayers," prayers that God doesn't answer the way we expected Him to. I can certainly think of a few prayers I'm glad God didn't answer my way, can't you? Prayer is not about changing God's mind; it's about changing *our* mind in light of how God wants things to happen. It's not about getting my will done on earth; it's about seeing His will done on earth as it is in heaven.

O Lord, teach us to pray.

AT THE FEET OF THE MASTER

God is not a vending machine we plug words into like coins in a slot, expecting answered prayers to come out at the bottom. Prayer is a discipline that must be learned and practiced. That's why the disciples petitioned Jesus, "Lord, teach us to pray" (Luke 11:1). Since prayer is such a prominent theme in the gospel of Luke, we know that Jesus had already been teaching His followers how to pray by example. We read, for instance, that "He often withdrew to deserted places and prayed" (5:16), sometimes spending "all night in prayer" (6:12), being in the habit of "praying in private" (9:18). They also knew that John's disciples had been taught to pray. It was common for rabbis, religious leaders, and prophets to teach their followers to pray. They learned by observing and listening. After seeing Jesus and knowing about John's disciples, these men concluded there was something missing in their lives—an understanding of prayer.

John had to teach his disciples to pray because of how corrupt the religious system had become. Remember, there had been four hundred years of silence between the last words of Malachi and the announcement of the birth of Christ. John needed to teach his disciples to move beyond the rote repetition of catch phrases, back to the true heart of prayer. Also, as the forerunner to Messiah, he must have surely taught them to pray expectantly for the soon coming Son of God.

The disciples did not ask Jesus to teach them how to perform miracles, how to multiply loaves and fish or to heal the sick. They didn't ask Him to give them a class in hermeneutics. They didn't want instructions in preaching, video presentations, drama, skits, or any aid to worship. They wanted to learn to pray. They had come to the conclusion on their own that the power behind the Person was prayer.

I believe today's American Christian talks a lot more about prayer than he or she actually prays. We are so busy, we have little time to be still and know that He is God. But through prayer we learn something about God and ourselves that we can't learn anywhere else.

One study says the average American spends twenty-eight hours a week in front of the television. Yet I doubt if the total hours spent by the average Christian in *prayer* each week would be more than one or two—if any!—even though prayer is the one thing the disciples asked to learn above all others. If Jesus' disciples needed to learn to pray, and if Jesus needed to get alone to pray, then we certainly need to spend time in prayer.

MORE THAN WORDS

Prayer is an admission of surrender, desperation, and weakness—an acknowledgment that I am not in charge of my life, that I am yielding my will to His. If I think I can live without having a consistent prayer life (and I have done it far too often), then I will never grow in my communion with the Father. Communion is a conversation that requires constant attention. God draws near to those who draw near to Him.

I am a big fan, for lack of a better term, of Pastor Jim Cymbala. What God has done through him at the Brooklyn Tabernacle cannot be explained in human terms. This church is an incredible place to visit, but I've always wanted to attend one of their prayer meetings. In fact, I am told that members will say if you have to miss on Sunday, don't miss prayer meeting. Brooklyn Tabernacle is a vibrant testimony of what can happen in a praying church.

Our minister of music, Mark Willard, and his wife, Katy, were at Brooklyn Tab a few years ago. They said it was one of the most powerful services they had ever been a part of. The singing was so loud and strong, they couldn't even hear each other. There is something about being clean before God and seeking His face that makes our singing sweeter. When I have spent time with God, getting my heart right before Him, I want to praise Him.

In the fall of 1994, Jim Cymbala wrote an article entitled "How to Light the Fire: What Does It Take to Motivate People to Pray?" In the article he relates this story:

> I walked into our empty, little sanctuary and recited to God a list of my problems: "Look at this building, this neighborhood. . . . Our offerings are laughable. . . . I can't trust so-and-so. . . . There's so little to work with." Then the Holy Spirit impressed upon me, "I will show you the biggest problem in the church. It's you." In that moment I saw with excruciating clarity that I didn't really love the people as God wanted me to. I prepared sermons just to get through another Sunday. I was basically prayerless. I was proud.[5]

I confess that seasons in my ministry could be defined as prayerless. When I study the lives of great men and women of faith, I wonder if I have even obtained a kindergarten degree in the school of prayer. Although one of the strongest influences in my early Christian life was the prayer meetings we had as a youth group, I can still lapse into times when I don't give concentrated time to prayer.

Jesus asked His disciples, "Couldn't you stay awake with Me one hour?" (Matt. 26:40). We have no problem with a three-hour ball game, but one hour in church is hard for some of us, much less one hour in prayer. There is no aspect of the Christian life more neglected than prayer.

We start to pray as we go to bed, and we fall asleep just after saying, "Dear God, I . . ." Our words lack meaning because they lack heart and focus. Someone has said, "Where there is no heart, there is no prayer." We eat, drink, sleep, go to work, attend various activities, even go to Bible studies, but we can still find ourselves rarely if ever speaking to God. Or we make prayer nothing more than a mindless repetition of words. The danger in thinking the Model Prayer is meant to be merely repeated verbatim is that it can become a meaningless formula. The Model Prayer is not a magic hocus-pocus incantation for recitation. It is a model, a guide, a pattern, a how-to.

In fact, the prayer in Luke's gospel is different from the one in Matthew's gospel, indicating that Jesus probably said these words on more than one occasion and didn't use the exact same words the second time. This seems to be a logical conclusion. Just as He healed people in different ways, Jesus did not pray the same words in every instance. When we do get insight into His prayers in various Scripture passages, they are different. His prayer in Luke 11, for example, is far different from the one He prayed in the Garden of Gethsemane.

John Calvin wrote, "It was not the intention of the Son of God . . . to prescribe the words which we must use, so as not to leave us at liberty to depart from the form which he has dictated. His intention, rather, was to guide and restrain our wishes that they might not go beyond those limits, and hence we infer that the rule which He has given us for praying aright relates not to the words, but to the things themselves."[6]

COME AGAIN

After presenting the Model Prayer, Jesus began speaking to His disciples in a parable.

> Suppose one of you has a friend and goes to him at midnight and says to him, "Friend, lend me three loaves of bread, because a friend of mine on a journey has come to me, and I don't have anything to offer him." Then he will answer from inside and say, "Don't bother me! The door is already locked, and my children and I have gone to bed. I can't get up to give you anything." I tell you, even though he won't get up and give him anything because he is his friend, yet because of his persistence, he will get up and give him as much as he needs. (Luke 11:5–8)

If you have ever traveled to the Holy Land, you know how hot it can be. There are few shade trees and a lot of rocks. The sun can beat down on you and drain your strength. So it wasn't uncommon in Jesus' day for people to do their traveling at night to avoid the heat of the day. It was also considered rude in that culture to turn someone away when they came to your door. Hospitality, then as now in the Middle East, was considered a sacred duty. And because bread was made daily, with only enough baked for the day's use, there was rarely any left over. Therefore, the late knock at the door from the traveler presented the man of the house with both an opportunity and a responsibility.

Having nothing himself, he went next door to see if he might find bread for his unexpected guest, knocking with shameless persistence. Faced with a need and no bread, he went to one whom he believed had some. The constant rapping on the door finally forced the neighbor to get out of bed. The Greek word for "persistence" is only found here in the New Testament. It's a word that means both shamelessness and boldness. There is nothing timid or withdrawn in this kind of knocking—or this kind of praying.

I was in Salt Lake City in October 2008 for the Utah/ Idaho Southern Baptist Pastors' Conference, serving as a guest preacher along with Tom Elliff. On the first day I heard Tom preach on this passage from Luke 11. Tom has served as a pastor, foreign missionary, and president of the Southern Baptist Convention. He is one of my favorite preachers, and I took notes as fast as I could while he was preaching, knowing I was working on this chapter. Tom described this scene by saying, "He went knocking on the door of his friend. He was actually testing his friendship and, by asking, seeking, and knocking, he was saying, 'I know you are too good of a friend to not give me what I need.' This was not vain repetition. These were the cries of a desperate man." I loved the way Tom illustrated this, painting the picture of a man standing there with his hands to his mouth, looking up and shouting, "Hey! Hey! Hey! I need some bread. Hey! Hey! Help me here!" Shameless persistence. Desperate seeking. Bold knocking.

The reason we need to be persistent in prayer is not because God is reluctant but because we tend to be lazy in our praying. We rarely are desperate enough to grab hold and not let go. We've all prayed for things and were indifferent regarding God's response. Persistence makes up its mind to state the case and the need boldly. "Hey God! I'm still here. Still asking. Still seeking. Still knocking."

Remember, the disciples had asked Jesus to teach them to pray, and He gave them this parable to encourage them to persevere in prayer. They needed to learn the principle of praying without ceasing—to pray and faint not. As the original languages indicate, "Ask and keep on asking. Seek and keep on seeking. Knock and keep on knocking." The atmosphere and aroma of our lives is to be that of prayer.

A GIVING FATHER

It would be a misinterpretation of this text to assume that our God has to be begged or that He is unwilling to help us unless coerced or arm-twisted. Jesus' parables were given to illustrate a truth, and they could be based either on contrast or likeness. This particular parable is used as a contrast, understood from the standpoint of the one knocking, not from the one who was awakened and responded reluctantly to the knock at the door. God is not reluctant; He is a giver. God is not deaf; He hears our cries. God is not resistant; He wants all to come to repentance. He hears the cries of the brokenhearted.

I'm a father. I want to give good things to my two girls. I say to people, "I've never considered taking my kids on a nice vacation an expenditure. I consider it an investment." I always go over our budget for Christmas because I'm always finding one more thing I want to give them. It's an expression of how much I love them as their dad.

As a parent I've always wanted to give my kids stuff. They would always go through a toy store and say, "I want this and that . . . and that over there . . . and this one . . . and one in that color." The reality is, as best I could, I gave them what they asked for at Christmas or their birthdays. But sometimes I gave them something they didn't ask for or beyond what they asked for.

I have a tender heart when it comes to my two daughters. I want God's best for them. I believe I'm their biggest fan. Terri and I are grateful for what God has done and is doing in them as young adult women. I can look back over times when we did that little something extra, not because they persisted but because we wanted to. For instance, my girls love New York City. So one year we decided to take a trip to New York at Christmastime.

I knew which shows they wanted to see, but I wanted to do more than just go, get a hotel, and see the shows. My wife is the trip planner in our family, so I asked her to set us up a trip to remember. When we arrived at the airport, a limo was there to get us. I wanted my girls to have their first limo ride with *me!* We stayed at the Plaza Hotel. We booked the cheapest room they had, but it was still the Plaza! They loved it. We ate at Tavern on the Green in Central Park. We went to shows, shopped, and ate at all the hot spots. I bought the best theater tickets I could get because our first trip to NYC as a family needed to be a great one. It was a memorable trip and one I was grateful to give them. On Christmas Eve we went to the Brooklyn Tabernacle for their Christmas service and musical. On Christmas Day we went to Radio City Music Hall for their Christmas show. We had Christmas brunch at the Plaza. It was a spread fit for a king.

I believe that's what God wants to do. He is not trying to see how little He can do for us. He longs to show us the "little something extra"—the extra touch, the extra blessing, the extra extravagance—just because He can. We rob ourselves of these blessings when we fail to love Him and seek Him. Persistence pays better than we can imagine.

And He doesn't just give stuff—He gives Himself! He is a giving and loving God. When I am thirsty, He is Living Water. When I am hungry, He is the Bread of Life. When I am weary, He is my strength. When I am confused, He gives me a renewed mind as I read His Word. God has told me and urged me to boldly approach the throne of grace to find help in time of need.

William Barclay says, "We are not wringing gifts from an unwilling God, but going to one who knows our needs better than we know them ourselves and whose heart towards us is the heart of generous love. If we do not receive what we pray for, it is not because God grudgingly refuses to give it, but because he has some better thing for us."[7]

The lesson is clear: Our praying should be persistent even when the answer doesn't come quickly. It's not that God is reluctant, needing convincing to change His mind. He is willing and ready to answer, but because of the apathy in our hearts, we are often flippant in our requests. We don't want to understand God's heart; we just want Him to get us out of a bind.

The persistent man in Jesus' parable refused to take no for an answer. His neighbor didn't want to get out of bed and give him bread, but he did want the man to stop pounding at the door, lest he wake up the kids. So he roused himself and gave the man what he asked for. The persistent petitioner was driven by the need of a late-night friend. He was also driven to go to someone who could help. As a parent, are you driven to the heavenly Father for wisdom, discernment, and guidance? As a believer, do you pray more for your needs, or for the needs of others? Is your "me" list longer than your "them" list?

God is not indifferent or apathetic toward our requests or our needs. The Lord is not a distant deity, nor is He asleep with a "Do Not Disturb" sign on the doors of heaven. God loves a cheerful giver because He Himself is a cheerful giver. He gave His Son. The Son gave Himself and left us the Holy Spirit.

"So I say to you, keep asking, and it will be given to you. Keep searching, and you will find. Keep knocking, and the door will be opened to you. For everyone who asks receives, and the one who searches finds, and to the one who knocks, the door will be opened" (Luke 11:9–10). These verses are a reminder that ceaseless prayer should characterize our lives, not just when we face a crisis. Too much of our praying is crisis praying, and not enough of it is meant to maintain and nurture the relationship with our heavenly Father.

Like any father, our heavenly Father doesn't always give us what we want when we want it. There are prayers God has not answered the way I wanted them answered. I've prayed for folks to be healed, and yet they've gone on to glory. I've prayed for people to come back into fellowship with God, but they are still in the distant land. God's delays must not be considered His denials. We shouldn't stop praying just because we don't get what we want when we want it.

The story is told of Sir Walter Raleigh going before Queen Elizabeth to ask her a large favor. The queen became exasperated and said, "Oh, Raleigh, when will you leave off begging?" His response was, "When your Majesty leaves off giving." Why do we ask, seek, and knock? Because these

> **OUR PRAYING SHOULD BE PERSISTENT EVEN WHEN THE ANSWER DOESN'T COME QUICKLY.**

three metaphors indicate something about the kind of praying our heavenly Father expects from us, and He has proven Himself willing to give.

BIGGER, BETTER GIFTS

Jesus goes on to state the case for persistent praying with another illustration. "What father among you, if his son asks for a fish, will give him a snake instead of a fish? Or if he asks for an egg, will give him a scorpion? If you then, who are evil, know how to give good gifts to your children, how much more will the heavenly Father give the Holy Spirit to those who ask Him? (Luke 11:11–13).

This is what the Hebrew rabbis call an argument from the lesser to the greater. The assumption is that if the first is true (vv. 11–12), then the second will be true to an even greater extent (v. 13). If we will give good things to our children and we are sinners by nature, how much more will our holy, loving, heavenly Father give to us? However generous and kind we think we are when it comes to our kids, we are nothing compared to our heavenly Father. As humans we are selfish by nature, but God is gracious and extravagant in His giving.

Jesus makes a point I believe is often missing when people talk about these verses. These words are spoken prior to the coming of the Holy Spirit in Acts. But Jesus says, "How much more will the heavenly Father give the Holy Spirit to those who ask Him?" I believe the disciples remembered this parable in those uncertain days following the Resurrection and prior to Pentecost. I believe as they gathered in that upper room, they probably said, as Tom Elliff would say, "Hey! Hey! Hey! You said you would send Your Spirit. He is the gift You promised to us—the power You promised. Hey! When is He coming? Hey! We're praying. We're ready. Send Him on down!"

The best gift you ever received was the Holy Spirit. Nothing more beautifully or lavishly expresses the love that God has for His children. Right now we have the Spirit of God living in us, praying for us, guiding us, and filling us. This being the case, why would God be reluctant to give anything else?

My dear friend Steve Williams is a deacon in our church, chairman of our personnel committee, and a wise counselor in my life. He played the role of Larry Childers in the Sherwood Pictures film *Facing the Giants*, the disabled father who encouraged his football kicker son to persevere through his fears. God has used Steve mightily in the last few years, but it has not been without some asking, seeking, and knocking. Read his story in his own words:

> On October 24, 2003, I was informed that my job had been eliminated as the result of a restructuring effort. Basically this meant that due to consolidation by the company, my almost fifteen-year career as a management employee suddenly came to an end. This news came as a total shock to me and was delivered without detailed explanation in a short meeting with a VP and an HR manager. There was no "thanks" for your contribution over the years or any going-away dinner plans, just "It's over and here's the paperwork!" I was about to turn fifty-three, and the thought of entering the job market was pretty overwhelming.
>
> I went straight home and told my wife, Becky. I'm sure I was still in a daze as I explained what had happened. I knew this probably was

not uncommon in today's business environment, but I never dreamed it could happen to me. Becky was stunned as well, and we just sat down and let the reality of it sink in for a few minutes. We shared a good cry and then prayed together. I immediately called my pastor Michael Catt and shared what happened. He suggested we get together right away, for which I am so grateful. As we met over lunch, he listened, offered words of encouragement, and prayed for me at a time when I was totally blown away by my circumstances. He also brought a great book for me by Ron Dunn, entitled *Surviving Friendly Fire*.

The next few days and weeks were filled with great emotional pain and some sleepless nights. Many friends called offering great encouragement and kind words of moral support, although others I felt certain would call me never did. Becky and our two grown children were beside me all the way with reassuring prayers and words of encouragement. The enemy followed up almost immediately, bringing feelings of anger, bitterness, failure, and great discouragement. I felt I had been grossly mistreated and dealt a great injustice. I was frustrated and angry, but didn't really know what to do about it.

While reading the book by Ron Dunn, I came across something that really hit home with me. In Exodus 14:14, Moses told the people being pursued by the Egyptians, "The Lord will fight for you, you need only to be still." It reminded me that justice belongs to God, and He will see to administering it. God was saying to me, "Forget those feelings of anger and resentment toward individuals. Focus instead on Me and what I have for you." When I grasped this truth, the negative feelings began to subside.

I read my Bible daily and prayed more fervently than ever. At first my prayers mostly consisted of asking God why this happened and to help me find a good job. I noticed while in this state of intense prayer, things began to happen. God became more real to me than ever before. I sensed His presence and felt His reassurance as I read the words of Scripture containing His promises about provision and protection for the believer. I felt the prayers of others begin to change my heart and lift my spirit. Feelings of discouragement and failure began to move further and further away. My worship was more real and sincere. The words of the pastor's messages seemed to all be coming right at me. Tears flowed freely as I sang the words of praise and worship songs at church and let the Holy Spirit fill my heart. I found myself often at the altar for prayer and meditation. My spiritual sensitivity was higher than ever.

At this point I was still mainly asking God to let me get back to this job I loved so much. I pursued several avenues for new opportunities and even had a few job interviews, but none really worked out. My wife and I prayed that we wouldn't have to relocate with a new job. We both loved our church where I was involved in teaching and leadership. We wanted to see come to fruition all that we believed God had for our church. But I also knew I needed a job. I knew that moving might be a reality. After about six weeks I was offered a great position with a major national company that required relocation. I also interviewed with a young and growing company for a position I could do without relocating but with some travel. The interview went great, but no offer came. We continued to pray for God's guidance in accepting the position that had been offered.

I began to feel that somehow my prayers for the right job were missing the mark. Soon I began to pray, "Lord, what do You want me to learn from this experience?" Almost instantly it came to me. The reason why this was so hard on me was because I had far too much value and pride associated with my former position. God revealed to me that my real value was not to be found in work or position but in who I was in Him. If my value was in my position or job title and I couldn't do it any longer, would I have no value? That's exactly how worthless I felt after my employment was terminated. But I began to realize how overvalued my former job was to me. It became clear that my focus should be on my influence as a believer upon my family and others. While I still needed a good job to pay my bills, enjoy a certain lifestyle, and be fulfilled vocationally, work was never to dominate or define my life again. My focus was to be on the difference I could make as a believer in the lives of others around me.

Time was slipping by as the year's end approached. I needed to make a decision on accepting the one solid job offer I had. I began to have an overwhelming feeling that somehow all was going to work out for the best. I now felt strengthened and spiritually renewed. On Christmas Eve, just four days before the deadline on the initial job offer, I received a call from the president of the company I had hoped would allow me to work and remain in Albany. He offered me a position with a total package much better than the first offer with no relocation required. God had answered our prayers once I began to seek not just another job but to seek what He had for me to learn through this very difficult situation.

It was through this unexpected crisis that a breakthrough occurred in my spiritual life. I am convinced fervent prayer was at the core of this spiritual revival. Once I realized God allowed this crisis for a reason and His desire for my life was a closer and deeper walk with Him, I knew it would all work out for the best (Rom. 8:28). I can now say that I know God as Jehovah Jireh, my provider. He has provided abundantly for me and my family by giving us the desires of our hearts. We remain active in our church, investing in the ministry of future generations. I was able to have a very spiritually rewarding experience as a cast member in the movie *Facing the Giants*. Within a year and half of my job change, both my children and five grandchildren moved back to Albany where we all worship together on Sundays. God graciously gives me the privilege of investing spiritually into their lives, as well as in others. My new job is much less stressful and very rewarding. Prayer is powerful. God's provision is abundant, and I am eternally grateful!

CHAPTER 5

WHEN YOU DON'T KNOW WHAT TO PRAY

Matthew 6

Because God is the living God, he can hear; because he is a loving God, he will hear; because he is our covenant God, he has bound himself to hear.
—C. H. Spurgeon

If you then, who are evil, know how to give good gifts to your children, how much more will your Father in heaven give good things to those who ask Him!
—Matthew 7:11

HAVE YOU EVER HAD one of those situations where you weren't sure what to pray? It happens all the time. We see a loved one lying in a coma and wonder if we should pray for God to take them or heal them. We're faced with an important decision, but we can't tell whether our prayers are self-centered or truly Christ-centered. We sometimes just have to hope we're praying correctly.

I remember feeling this way when my mom was dying. As I related in my book *Prepare for Rain*, I didn't find out until age thirty-nine that I was adopted. For whatever reason, this unexpected development caused me to struggle mightily with anger and an unwillingness to forgive. I fought to grasp and understand why I had not been told earlier. Over time, however, I embraced the fact that God is sovereign and I'm not. I learned to rejoice in the fact that He had placed me in a Christian home and that I had been raised in the church. I learned to praise Him for not letting my birth mom have a back-alley abortion.

> **WHEN WE PRAY, GOD PUTS ON OUR HEART WHAT IS ON HIS HEART.**

At the same time, I was trying to decide if I should ever confront my parents with what I had found out. What would it do to them in their later years? Would it answer my questions at the expense of causing wounds to their hearts?

Over the last few months of her life, my mother had apparently lost her will to live. As she slipped into a diabetic coma, I was called home to be nearby in her final hours. After my father and I made the difficult DNR decision ("Do Not Resuscitate"),

I went back to the ICU to spend a few moments with Mom by myself. Sitting by her bedside, I held her hand and told her that I knew about the adoption. I told her how grateful I was for her and that it was OK with me. I wasn't sure exactly what to say, but I found my words forming a prayer of grace, forgiveness, and moving forward. I wasn't there a long time, but I do believe God heard my heart.

He always does—even when we don't know what to pray.

WHEN PRAYERS GO WRONG

When you don't know what to pray, the Model Prayer is a good place to start. In Matthew 6, we find our Lord dealing with three significant issues—giving, praying, and fasting—but the greatest emphasis is on prayer. It seems as if the Lord was teaching us how to read the Bible in context, how to synthesize the various disciplines of our Christian life into a unified whole.

Giving, for example, is a big part of our responsibility as believers. I believe one reason God can't bless some folks is because they are disobedient in the realm of giving. Yet I've heard people justify not tithing or supporting the church by saying, "I've prayed about it," feeling sure the Bible doesn't really call for this, as though God is exempting them from needing to comply to a clear command of Scripture. But since when did the Holy Spirit ever violate the written Word of God in response to our prayers? When we pray, God puts on our heart what is on His heart. Therefore, biblical giving (like biblical fasting) comes out of a vital prayer life. They are meaningless apart from prayer.

The Jewish people have always been very serious about prayer. Many of the Psalms are prayers. Scripture contains great laments offered during times of suffering when the people cried out to God to understand what was going on. So over the course of time, the religious leaders determined they had prayer down to a science. They had God all figured out. But their prayers had become little more than rote and recitation. They lacked power and weren't getting through to God. That's why Jesus said:

> Whenever you pray, you must not be like the hypocrites, because they love to pray standing in the synagogues and on the street corners to be seen by people. I assure you: They've got their reward! But when you pray, go into your private room, shut your door, and pray to your Father who is in secret. And your Father who sees in secret will reward you. When you pray, don't babble like the idolaters, since they imagine they'll be heard for their many words. Don't be like them, because your Father knows the things you need before you ask Him. (Matt. 6:5–8)

I once heard someone pray, "Lord, forgive us our prayers." Have you ever been in a prayer meeting where someone just rambles on and on, like what 1 Corinthians 13 refers to as a "tinkling cymbal"? Have you weathered the storm of a saint who is obviously impressed with the sound of his own voice when he prays? This was what the Pharisees did. They prayed with no other purpose than to be seen and heard. Jesus spoke of this in Luke 18 when He compared the self-righteous Pharisee and the humble, self-effacing publican. Prayers don't have to sound pious to be profound. It's not really prayer if your goal is to impress others with your words, phrases, and petitions.

Jesus also condemned meaningless repetition, as if God didn't hear us the first time. This is the kind of praying pagans do, He said. They jump up and down and go through all these meaningless rituals and phrases, hoping their idol will respond. My favorite example of this was the false prophets of Baal during the time of Elijah. They prayed, cut themselves, and cried out to their gods to pay attention. Jesus said, "My followers don't have to do that."

James Montgomery Boice, in his insightful commentary on Matthew, writes:

> Jesus is not condemning long prayers in these verses since he himself spent long nights and many hours in prayer. What he is condemning is "vain repetition," a phrase that came into the King James Version by way of Theodore Beza's commentary. The Greek word is *battalogeo* (v. 7), probably from the Aramaic *battal*, meaning "idle." It is a warning against vain words in praying. Sadly, many religious prayers are like this. Indeed, we can even be idle in our repetition of the so-called Lord's Prayer, which

follows these verses. We should remember that the slang term "pitter-patter" in English comes from the Latin words that begin the Lord's Prayer (*Pater Noster*) and are an observation on how meaningless the empty repetition of even these famous words has sometimes seemed to unbelievers. Augustine was on the right track when he properly distinguished between much speaking in prayer and much praying.[1]

Historians and commentators tell us that a pious Jew would pray three times a day, and their prayers would include eighteen petitions. Their normal memorized prayer was about three times longer than this Model Prayer. Jesus taught His followers that the spirit of a prayer is more important than the length or words used. This is a pattern, not a law. The Model Prayer is the skeleton in our personal praying; we put the meat on the bones. It's the framework; we have to add the body to it.

In 1990 the late Lehman Strauss did a Bible conference at our church. I remember one session in which he talked about this idea of lengthy prayers. He had been a guest speaker at a conference where a certain man was called on to say the blessing before the noon meal. He said the man prayed them from Egypt to Canaan. And when they finally got to the Promised Land, the food was cold. And he never actually asked God to bless the meal!

Jesus told us not to pray "like the hypocrites," which means we shouldn't even get caught in the trap of using catchwords or phrases when we pray. Prayer is a conversation between the children of God and their Father. As children, we didn't go to our dads and say, "O great and awesome father who gave life to this worthless child, who sits on the checkbook which, if released, would allow me to buy the latest gadget at the mall, who knows that I am in need of an increase in my allowance. Be benevolent to me, O great Father of whom I am not worthy. Grant to me, in thy great kindness and grace, a few more dollars that I might purchase the items for which I am currently interceding. Do not let me leave your presence, Dad of all dads, without your blessings or your credit card. If you will but just see things my way, I will forever call you blessed and will determine in my heart to give you a better card this Father's Day." And that's not how we should pray either.

We go to our dads, knowing they love us, but also knowing they have our best interest in mind. We make our requests in light of relationship. We don't have to say "dad" or "father" at the beginning of every sentence. We should know who we're talking to. Repeating "dad" or "father" over and over is not necessary. Jesus is trying to teach us that conversation with our heavenly Father is to be a natural response in light of an intimate relationship. Stephen Charnock said, "All the prayers in the Scripture you will find to be reasoning with God, not a multitude of words heaped together."

Throughout the Bible we find twenty-three prayers of Jesus. In addition to His regular times of prayer, we find Him praying at His baptism, when He selected the Twelve, at the Transfiguration, at the feeding of the five thousand, at the raising of Lazarus, at Gethsemane, at the cross, and at His ascension. Look at all the areas covered by these prayers. They reveal that Jesus prayed when He was alone or in a crowd. He prayed to His Father at the greatest moments as well as the darkest moments of His life. He prayed at the beginning of His earthly ministry and at the end.

When Jesus taught His disciples how to pray, He didn't tell them, "Just learn these words, guys, and you'll get whatever you want." The Model Prayer is not a prayer to be memorized, nor is it a prayer to manipulate the will of God. Some denominations pray the Model Prayer—the Lord's Prayer—in every service. I sometimes wonder how many actually mean what they are saying and praying. Or are they just saying words that have long since lost any meaning and power in their lives?

This is a prayer focused first and foremost on the glory, honor, and will of God. All praying must begin there, or else it devolves into self-centeredness. Although we are told to approach Him as Father, this does not give us permission to be chummy with the Almighty. There's a difference between intimacy and irreverence. Remember who you're talking to.

MODELING PRAYER

In the fifty-five words of the Model Prayer (give or take a few depending on the translation or gospel you're reading), we find volumes of material to instruct us in what to pray when our words fall short. Look at the difference in how Jesus taught us to pray. This prayer is short, simple, and to the point. It is a prayer that many of us memorized as children, yet the depths of this prayer take a lifetime to extract. We are commanded to pray and to pray in secret.

> Our Father in heaven,
> Your name be honored as holy.
> Your kingdom come.
> Your will be done on earth as it is in heaven.
> Give us today our daily bread.
> And forgive us our debts, as we also have forgiven our debtors.
> And do not bring us into temptation, but deliver us from the evil one.
> For Yours is the kingdom and the power and the glory forever. Amen.
> (Matt. 6:9–13)

In his book *Sense and Nonsense about Prayer*, Lehman Strauss writes: "The prayer contains six petitions. The first three have to do with God and His glory; the last three relate to man and his needs. This is the divine order for proper praying, and it cannot be reversed. In true prayer, God and His glory claim top priority. Selfishness and self-centeredness are out. Everything the Christian does should be for the glory of God (1 Cor. 10:31), and prayer is the Christian's highest exercise."[2]

As you examine this prayer, you will discover it's selflessness. Most importantly, the eternal takes precedence over that which is earthly. What God wants is more important than what we want.

- It's a model for all, not just for the elite ("Our Father in heaven").
- It's a model of reverence in the presence of God ("Your name be honored as holy").
- It's a model of surrender to His lordship ("Your will be done").
- It's a model for the abiding life ("Give us . . .").
- It's a model of the relationship between prayer and forgiveness ("Forgive us . . .").

Few if any think of the Model Prayer in terms of ministry focus. In fact, unless you are a member of a more liturgical church, I doubt your church prays the Model Prayer in any corporate gathering. Again, this can become rote and ritual. It can lose its meaning over time, much like singing the same songs each week can become redundant. However, I am more convinced than ever that the failure of the church and her leaders to pray in accordance with the Model Prayer is the reason our churches are so ineffective. I read books about how to change a church or grow a church, but there are very few books about how to get a church to pray.

In this age of "size means substance," we have forgotten that Jesus did more with twelve than some of our churches are doing with twelve hundred or twelve thousand. Those few did more to impact their world than we are doing to impact ours. Why? We don't know how to pray. And when we do actually pray, we often just pray the announcements. Rarely do you see today's tight, packaged worship service featuring an emphasis on prayer. Seeing people with their heads bowed in reverence to God isn't good television, I guess. Airtime is expensive, so it's more important for people to see our lights, hear our sermonettes for Christianettes, and listen to a great band than to hear us crying out to God.

Rarely do we call people to the altar to pray. Why? We've got the program lined out. The form is fixed and the order is set. Who has time to pray? The preacher needs time to preach. The worship team needs time to sing their songs. We don't have time to pray. If we do, it's only to ask God to stir people's hearts as we take the offering.

But if this is the Model Prayer, maybe it should be the model for how we lead our churches as well. Is there a reverence for God in your worship? If you took away the coffee and doughnuts in Sunday school, would they still come? Is there a time when you mention more than the hospital list in your church prayer time? Is there a surrender to His lordship in our lives? Is it *His* church or *our* church—or the *pastor's* church? Is there a sense of abiding and abounding, or is it more about rushing from one thing to the next? Is there a spirit of forgiveness, or are our pews filled with people who are angry, bitter, hurt, and unwilling to let go of the past?

I've been to more church growth conferences than I care to remember. But rarely have I been to a conference where prayer was more than a passing thought. Due to this lack of praying, my first priority at Sherwood was to establish an intercessory prayer ministry. I wanted the focus of this membership to be on intercessory prayer.

As a result of Don Miller speaking about prayer at Sherwood in 1990, the congregation committed to building a prayer chapel. The first one was located outside my office, and today that chapel has been moved to our high school campus. When we moved into our new worship facility, we built a new two-story prayer tower at the front of our church property. It has an upper room as well as two prayer closets downstairs. Every day, members of Sherwood go in to pray over the needs of others.

I believe God has blessed us as a church family because of our emphasis on prayer, because of our deliberate focus on the fact that He is our God, our provider, our source of strength and wisdom. We often call the men of the church to the altar to pray over specific needs in our worship services. We pray for those in authority and for those serving our country. We pray for other churches.

> **IF WE WANT HIS WILL DONE ON EARTH AS IT IS IN HEAVEN, WE'VE GOT TO START PRAYING MORE.**

Oh, we've still got a long way to go, but if we want His will done on earth as it is in heaven, we've got to start praying more. And our praying needs to be more focused and effective. We've got all the programs and seminars we can handle. Our shelves are full of product, but our pews are lacking in power.

FIRST AND FOREMOST

I recently read a book on growing churches. The authors asked the pastors of these churches to rank the top ten reasons why their churches were growing. They mentioned things like exciting worship, good fellowship, target ministries, community outreach, relocation, and facilities, but not one of them listed prayer in their top ten. I believe, in the words of the old hymn, that "all is vain unless the Spirit of the Holy One comes down." We have size, but do we have substance? Substance comes when we're focused on biblical priorities. We have crowds, but are we building congregations?

In searching through my tape files, I found a message by Alan Redpath, once the pastor of the Moody Church in Chicago. He said, "The tendency for many Christians is to imagine that a church can be conducted and led in the same way as a business concern—publicity, propaganda, and a bright front. But the Church of Jesus Christ can only be led in blessing and power by men who have been humbled and broken at the cross, those who have been taught by the Holy Spirit to lay hold of Him at the throne of Grace."

You can't read the gospels without understanding the importance that Jesus put on prayer. You can't read the book of Acts without seeing overwhelming evidence that the early church embraced prayer as a priority. I would submit to you that their effectiveness in evangelism, missions, and church growth was the result of their prayer ministry.

You can't read the letters of Paul without seeing how praying for the church was strategic to his plan for spreading the gospel and growing the saints. Andrew Murray said, "Most churches don't know that God rules the world by the prayers of His saints." Could the missing ingredient in the twenty-first century church be prayer? It is pivotal in the Far East and underground churches, but prayer seems to be less important to the Western church. No wonder the gospel is growing in the East and dying in the West.

In Luke's gospel the disciples did not ask Jesus to give them the five steps to church growth. They didn't ask Him to help them design an ad campaign. They didn't talk to Him about how to raise a church budget and train leaders. They didn't ask Him to teach them how to heal or preach. They asked Him to teach them to pray. But what was first for them is unfortunately last for us.

Lord, teach us to pray!

I picked up a book in a used bookstore entitled *Ten Praying Churches*, a fascinating look at a handful of congregations in England who have taken prayer seriously. I was struck by the words in the foreword, written by Terry Virgo:

> Prayer must always be the distinctive feature of the house of God. When we make prayer a priority, we are telling God that we totally depend on him. We need his interventions and the manifestation of his presence and power. Without prayer we start trusting in our own ability and resourcefulness, and as we begin to trust in human skills and organising expertise, we lose the glory of God.
>
> By his own example, Jesus taught his disciples that prayer was crucial. They would have yielded to the demands of the crowds and to

other people's expectations, but Jesus refused every distraction. Later the apostles demonstrated that they had learned the lesson well by withdrawing from the clamour of the growing church and giving themselves to prayer.

The early church never regarded prayer meetings as dull routine—a duty to be performed and a proof of evangelical orthodoxy. In the Book of Acts the church at prayer was also the church in action. The Day of Pentecost started as a prayer meeting, but God broke in and they broke out. Who can tell from the narrative precisely when they moved from sitting in the house in prayer and came into the streets in power? The next recorded prayer meeting concludes not only with the building shaking but also with the disciples freshly filled with the Holy Spirit and power.

When Peter was taken to prison, the church's natural reflex action was to once again gather to pray, resulting in his miraculous release. When the church at Antioch met to pray, the meeting resulted in a breakthrough of missionary activity as the people released their leaders to advance the gospel to other lands.

The boredom often associated with prayer meetings in the past has been caused by their predictability and lack of living purpose. But if

churches are actively involved in works of faith
that require the presence of God, prayer will
become relevant and exciting.[3]

We have been offered the opportunity to boldly approach the God of heaven, but prayer meeting in most churches is the most poorly attended gathering of the week. Some have canceled prayer meeting altogether, while some prayer meetings have become nothing more than a recitation of the hospital report, having very little to do with the kind of praying we are told to do.

The clergy in the Church of England read prayers in the church every morning and evening, but only a handful if any ever hears them. The *Book of Common Prayer* has become so "common" that it's taken for granted. What's *uncommon* is to find a praying church. It is the exception, when biblically it should be the rule.

Our weekly prayer meetings are weak. What happened to the days when men like Spurgeon said that his prayer meeting on Monday nights rarely had less than a thousand to twelve hundred people present? Revivals are birthed in prayer. When God's people pray, God hears. Prayer is serious to God, but is it to us? Spurgeon said, "Because God is the living God, he can hear; because he is a loving God, he will hear; because he is our covenant God, he has bound himself to hear."

Have we not reduced God to a formula? We say, "Buy this book. Go to this conference. Repeat after me." We have conferences to teach young preachers how to preach, but we so rarely teach them how to pray. We have ladies' Bible studies where they dig into the Word, but few of these studies ever focus on the priority of prayer. If we have full heads and cold hearts, we are no better than the Pharisees. Jesus is not looking for better educated people. He is looking for biblically effective people.

In his "Be" commentary series, Warren Wiersbe points out, "It is worth noting that there are no singular pronouns in this prayer; they are all plural. It begins with "Our Father." When we pray, we must remember that we are part of God's worldwide family of believers. We have no right to ask for ourselves anything that would harm another member of the family. If we are praying in the will of God, the answer will be a blessing to all of God's people in one way or another."[4]

Are we not guilty of asking "our Father" to bless our church while failing to ask Him to bless other churches? The spirit of competition in the church is rampant. It's not just us against the world; it's us against the church down the street. We are more interested in gaining members than building the kingdom.

What if God sent a mighty wind of the Spirit through the church down the street? Would you be jealous? Would you point out all their faults and shortcomings? Or would you rejoice that "our Father" is pouring out a blessing on another member of our family? Praying the way Jesus teaches us to pray requires an unselfish spirit. My first priority and that of my church should be His kingdom, not my agenda.

The church that does not depend on the Father thinks it can make its own bread. It lacks a dependent spirit. Our Father is the only One who can provide bread in the wilderness. Too often our church work resembles a factory where we think we can churn out bread by the truckload. Yes, the world is indeed spiritually starving, but they aren't flocking to our doors for the bread we're offering. They need true bread—the Bread of Life— the One who turns our bread into something worth having.

LIVING IN ANOTHER WORLD

Because God is our Father, we have a right to pray, but we also have an obligation to pray. Prayer is a requirement. We are to be in constant communication with our Father, submitting ourselves to Him as sovereign and King. "Your kingdom come" means it's not about you or me. It's all about Him.

The Model Prayer, then, is a prayer of anticipation.

At the time of Jesus, kingdoms dominated the earth. Emperors had empires, monarchs had monarchies, and chieftains had tribes. But Jesus proclaimed the gospel of the kingdom. The purpose of this chapter is not to give the various theological interpretations of what the kingdom is or when it will come. Rather it is to remind us that as individuals, leaders, and churches, the kingdom is not ours, but His.

I often hear someone say, "That's Brother So-and-So's church," or "The so-and-so family runs that church." You can't be a praying pastor or a praying member and demand the church be about you. When Jesus is Lord, it means God has the right to exercise His sovereign power in you and through you.

Jesus made the kingdom a central image of what He came to accomplish. This image is used more than a hundred times in the New Testament. Paul said, "The kingdom of God is not eating and drinking, but righteousness, peace, and joy in the Holy Spirit" (Rom. 14:17). Eating and drinking is what kings did in that day. They planned feasts in their own honor and partied all night. The Scripture, however, gives us a new understanding of the kingdom. It is spiritual in nature, centered on Jesus Christ.

- Jesus proclaimed the kingdom to the crowd nine times.
- Sixteen times He said it must be entered.
- Four times He described it as an inheritance.
- Six times He said it was good news.
- Three times He said it was a secret revealed.
- He said it was like seed sown that yields a harvest.
- He described it as a mustard seed that grows into a tree.
- He called it yeast that leavens a lump of dough.
- He referred to it as a dragnet that captures many fish.
- He defined it as a great feast.

We find many pictures of the kingdom, but they all tell us something. There is a current reality and a future hope to this kingdom. It is here and it is also coming. Peter Lewis says, "When we pray, 'your kingdom come,' we should realize that we are praying about something very serious. We are praying about something that will be as terrible to some as it will be joyful to others. We are praying for the closing of the door as well as the opening of the gates; the final exclusion of the unbelieving, including the undecided, as well as the entrance of the redeemed and reconciled race into its destiny, the kingdom

prepared for it from the foundation of the world. We are praying for the end of the old order with its space for repentance as
well as its pain and its tears."

Today I fear that neither the average believer nor the average church is willing to pray in this way. We are too enamored
with "feel good" experiences to focus our attention on a coming
judgment. We have foolishly assumed that maybe if we don't
pray this way, things will all work out to our liking or God will
not do what He has predetermined to do.

Someone has said that right now we are "between the
times"—the season *after* the kingdom has come but before it
has *fully* come. In the meantime, then, we need to be serious
about where this world is headed. Serious times demand serious
praying. We see the adherents of other religions stop and pray
numerous times a day, facing toward a certain city. But we can't
even get Christians to pray before a meal at a local restaurant
because they're too embarrassed to live out their faith.

Jesus was clear when He said:

> Not everyone who says to Me, "Lord, Lord!"
> will enter the kingdom of heaven, but only the
> one who does the will of My Father in heaven.
> On that day many will say to Me, "Lord, Lord,
> didn't we prophesy in Your name, drive out
> demons in Your name, and do many miracles
> in Your name?" Then I will announce to them,
> "I never knew you! Depart from Me, you law-
> breakers!" (Matt. 7:21–23)

Note that Jesus ties together the proclamation of Himself as Lord with His Father in heaven. Fruit reveals both who we are and who we're following. No fruit, no root. Just going to church and wearing the T-shirt doesn't make you one of His. Just because the sign on the front of the building says "church" doesn't make you a church. There's a difference between lip service and lordship. I believe a church without vital prayer is ultimately just doing lip service. Most of the works, although done sincerely, could end up being wood, hay, and stubble.

Can we admit we need to evaluate our prayer lives and our prayer ministries? Churches are trying to figure out more and more ways to cut prayer so they can add new activities and fluff. Churches have eliminated prayer meetings and stopped having Sunday night services because people won't come. Sooner or later, I suppose, we won't need the church at all because the carnal won't even get up on Sunday mornings!

If put to the prayer test, most of what we do would not advance the kingdom or honor the King. Much of it is about entertaining the saints, giving the kids a place to hang out, and providing programs because parents are too lazy or too busy to be the spiritual leaders in their own homes. If God probed our churches, would He find people committed to His will, His kingdom, His Word, and His way? Or would He find little more than a baptized social club?

In *The Kingdom Focused Church*, Gene Mims writes:

> The kingdom has nothing to do with obscure doctrine or difficult rules. It's about living the

life that God intends for you to have. It is a life worth finding, a life worth living, and a life of genuine joy and excitement. Life in the kingdom of God is not a sheltered, careful life without risk, failure, achievement, or excitement. It's a life that's real in that everything we face is real. Life is filled with good and bad. We have joy alongside our sorrows and triumphs along with our defeats. Kingdom living is not an escape. It is an engagement. It is living at the highest human level even in the midst of the lowest human experience. It is full throttle, wide open, going straight ahead to an indescribable life.[5]

Exciting. Indescribable. Doesn't characterize much of our praying, does it? But it should. We think excitement in our lives or in the church comes through programs, events, concerts, plays, movies, drama, great press, or word-of-mouth. But those things are fleeting. Today's latest thing is yesterday's old news.

In these ever-changing times we are not told to keep up with the world. We are told to lay hold of God and ask Him to bring His kingdom into our world. If our churches were more kingdom-minded, we would be less success-oriented. We would measure less by numbers and more by knees on the floor in prayer. We would think less of promotion and more of longing for His manifest presence. We would die to our wills and live instead for His.

The test of our willingness to pray "Your Kingdom come, Your will be done" is found in the level of our obedience to His Word. It should be our desire in prayer to see the King and His kingdom, praying toward that day when He comes as King of kings and Lord of lords.

WE ARE NOT TOLD TO KEEP UP WITH THE WORLD. WE ARE TOLD TO LAY HOLD OF GOD AND ASK HIM TO BRING HIS KINGDOM INTO OUR WORLD.

PUT IT TO THE TEST

Think about the praying we do as individuals, in small groups, and as a church. Often it is self-absorbed. How easy it is to think only of our needs, desires, goals, and dreams. Even as adults we often act like crying babies, thinking the world revolves around us. When we finally do focus on others, we sometimes find ourselves praying only that the situation will work out the way we want it to—praying for our own best interests—rather than praying for God's plan and purpose. It's hard to lay our Isaac down. It's even harder to get on the altar and become a living sacrifice.

When we pray, "Your kingdom come, Your will be done," we are acknowledging that Christ is Lord and has no rivals. We call on the Lord of glory to accomplish and complete His work. We pray that His rule will be established. In a democracy like we have in America, we are partisan with our preconceived ideas of what would be best for our country. As citizens of heaven, however, we need to be focused on what is most in line with what God wants, what God says is best. We often seek His will for big situations and decisions, but how often do we seek Him in the seemingly little things? God wants His will done on earth as it is in heaven. Are we praying that way?

Steve Hale, a Southern Baptist evangelist, tells the story of an ordained accident in which God revealed His will in a very unusual way.

It was two weeks before our wedding, and I had not yet received any correspondence from the housing office of Southwestern Seminary, even though we had been on the housing list for more than six months. I was not too concerned, though, because I had been dropping by periodically to be sure we were still in line. The receptionist had always assured me I was number eight on the list. Yet a failure to receive written confirmation of this fact seemed a bit strange. So before leaving for Kentucky to tie the knot, I checked in one more time to be sure everything was in order.

This time, however, the man at the desk informed me he had no record of me being on Southwestern's housing file. I assured him that I was number eight on the list, as the woman had told me. He went back to review the list again, only to return with a negative answer. I persisted, "Sir, please go back and check under my full name, Charles Steven Hale."

When he returned the second time, he said, "Mr. Hale, I'm sorry, but you are not on our housing list." With a desperate tremble in my voice, I said to him, "Sir, I am getting married in two weeks, and my wife expects a roof over her head. Surely there is something you can do, isn't there?" Very matter-of-factly he replied, "No sir. You understand the over-crowded conditions of this institution. There is nothing we can do." It was obvious he did not have the spiritual gift of mercy.

With a pounding heart I called my mother in Kentucky and asked that she and Dad pray about this predicament. I recall kneeling beside the bed in my apartment, praying, "Oh God, I don't understand. Either You are trying to tell me that I am about to make the worst mistake of my life by marrying the wrong person. Or You are telling us that our wedding date is not in Your timing. Or You are getting ready to perform a miracle. I'm not asking for instant answers, but I do ask for Your peace."

That was on Saturday. The next day my mother called to say, "Steve, I don't know where you are to be living, but I was praying yesterday, and God gave me His peace that it's all under control." I said, "Mom, God gave me the same peace."

The very next morning I was stopped at a yield sign in Fort Worth, Texas, on Interstate 20. I looked in my rearview mirror and saw a car headed toward me with no intention of slowing down. I braced myself for impact. *Crash!* Then after the collision, the man who had smashed into my car ran over to ask if I was OK. Major damage had been done to the car, but while waiting for the police and wrecker to arrive at the scene, this complete stranger and I became acquainted. In the course of our conversation, I discovered he had a son who had graduated from Southwestern Seminary. I said, "I'm a student at Southwestern." His classic reply was, "Well, of all people to run into." Not funny.

Then this stranger asked if I was in a hurry to go anywhere. He indicated that he wanted to become better acquainted. As we were driving through the city, it occurred to me I had prayed that morning and said, "Lord, whatever the circumstances of this day are, I ask You to respond to them through me." Having remembered that prayer, I said, "Mr. Eitelman, do you know of any rental property in Fort Worth?" He said, "No, but you're praying about it. You keep praying and God will answer." That's not what I wanted to hear. Five minutes later he pulled the car into the driveway of a house

I had never seen before. Dust covered the furniture and cobwebs hung in the corners of the house, but it was nice. In fact, the house had three bedrooms, solid wood antique furniture, oriental rugs, genuine brass beds, a beautiful chandelier, and a nice fireplace with an antique mantel clock. After giving me the tour, this "stranger" walked back to the front porch and asked, "How do you like it?" I said, "This is very nice." He said, "It's yours."

What? His response startled me. "It's yours," he reaffirmed. I'm sure my mouth must have dropped wide open, but I asked, "How much rent are you asking?" He said, "None. All I ask is that you pay the utilities, and you may live here as long as you like."

What is the possibility of driving on the sophisticated interstate highway systems of the Dallas-Fort Worth metroplex and having a sixty-five-year-old man run into my car and give us a house, the very thing for which we had been praying? Some would say, "Sheer coincidence." But no, this is the power of the God we serve. Jeremiah 33:3 says, "Call unto Me and I will answer you and I will show you great and mighty things that you don't know about." God is saying, "I'm full of surprises, and I have resources that you know nothing about.

Trust Me and call upon Me." As an evangelist, I refer back to that day every so often. God is my Provider. Yes, some "accidents" are ordained by God.

We see things from a different perspective when we see them through prayer. We view life, our choices, our circumstances, and even those strange coincidences that come along from time to time through a different lens. Seeking the will of God in prayer is not about our agenda, our itinerary, or our calendar. It's about His agenda and what's on the eternal calendar. It is never about our schedule but about the *surrender* of our schedule. When we walk in the will of God, we cannot fail. But when we try to walk outside the will of God, we cannot succeed.

Thomas Aquinas said it well, "A man's heart is right when he wills what God wills." A. W. Tozer added, "To pray effectively we must want what God wants—that and that only is to pray in the will of God."

CHAPTER 6

WHEN YOU PRAY, HAVE FAITH AND . . .

Mark 11

Faith is the foundation of prayer, and prayer should be nothing else but faith exercised.
—Thomas Manton

Now this is the confidence we have before Him: whenever we ask anything according to His will, He hears us. And if we know that He hears whatever we ask, we know that we have what we have asked Him for.
—1 John 5:14–15

JAY STRACK, founder and president of Student Leadership University, is a dear friend. He is a visionary, an evangelist, and a cutting-edge thinker when it comes to reaching the next generation for Christ. Jay grew up in a difficult home situation, but God called him out and set him apart for unique ministry. I've asked him to share some of his story about the power of persistent praying and forgiveness.

> During a time of earnest and persistent prayer, the Lord spoke forcefully to me about forgiving a relative. In the past we had exchanged some very hurtful words; he had criticized my ministry and even demeaned my character. I was proud of the fact that I had made several attempts to reach out to him and felt the ball was in his court.
>
> But in the midst of pouring myself into the work and vision the Lord had given me, God stopped everything from moving forward. I persistently continued to pray, reflect, and inspect my life. I prayed the psalmist's words, "Search me, O God, and know my heart; try me, and know my anxieties; and see if there is any wicked way in me, and lead me in the way everlasting" (Psalm 139:24).
>
> God answered that prayer. I was given the assignment for a Bible conference to speak on the passage in Luke 17 about being quick to

forgive. I read this passage over and over. It is a direct command from Jesus to take the initiative and do everything in our power to resolve conflict, regardless of whether we have been the offender or the offended.

I have given up drugs. I have faced difficult uncertainties. But perhaps the most challenging thing I have had to do in my life was to humble myself. I knew I was to take the initiative, apologize for anything I had done, and restore the relationship as God intended. What began as one of the most difficult moments of my life quickly became one of the most liberating and most meaningful. I could literally feel the burden lift and those roots of bitterness pull up out of the soil of my heart. What I thought would be a haughty reaction was a tearful response.

I have learned from personal experience what I already knew to be true from the Scripture. When prayer according to the will of God is not answered, we must look to our own hearts for the problem. The two single greatest hindrances to answered prayer are broken and forgotten promises that we have made to the Father and a hardening of our own hearts. Fortunately for us, He is quicker to forgive than we are. When we ignore a hurting relationship, He pursues it until peace is found.

You can't read the gospels without finding a principle regarding faith and forgiveness in the prayers and teachings of Jesus. Consider these well-known passages:

> Forgive us our debts, as we also have forgiven our debtors. . . . For if you forgive people their wrongdoing, your heavenly Father will forgive you as well. But if you don't forgive people, your Father will not forgive your wrongdoing. (Matt. 6:12, 14–15)

> Peter came to Him and said, "Lord, how many times could my brother sin against me and I forgive him? As many as seven times?"
>
> "I tell you, not as many as seven," Jesus said to him, "but 70 times seven. For this reason, the kingdom of heaven can be compared to a king who wanted to settle accounts with his slaves. When he began to settle accounts, one who owed 10,000 talents was brought before him. Since he had no way to pay it back, his master commanded that he, his wife, his children, and everything he had be sold to pay the debt.
>
> "At this, the slave fell facedown before him and said, 'Be patient with me, and I will pay you everything!' Then the master of that slave had compassion, released him, and forgave him the loan. But that slave went out and

found one of his fellow slaves who owed him 100 denarii. He grabbed him, started choking him, and said, 'Pay what you owe!' At this, his fellow slave fell down and began begging him, 'Be patient with me, and I will pay you back.' But he wasn't willing. On the contrary, he went and threw him into prison until he could pay what was owed.

When the other slaves saw what had taken place, they were deeply distressed and went and reported to their master everything that had happened. Then, after he had summoned him, his master said to him, 'You wicked slave! I forgave you all that debt because you begged me. Shouldn't you also have had mercy on your fellow slave, as I had mercy on you?' And his master got angry and handed him over to the jailers until he could pay everything that was owed. So My heavenly Father will also do to you if each of you does not forgive his brother from his heart." (Matt. 18:21–35)

If I claim to be a person of faith, I must also be a person who forgives. Ron Dunn's book on faith left me with an indelible understanding that faith and forgiveness are inseparable. There have been moments when I wanted God to do something great in my life, only to be reminded by the Holy Spirit that I had something against a brother or sister in Christ.

DOES FAITH GROW ON TREES?

I want to focus on a passage in Mark 11—a pivotal passage in the fast-paced account of Mark's gospel. This was the last day of Jesus' public ministry. He had spent the night in Bethany at the home of Mary, Martha, and Lazarus, and was headed back into Jerusalem. On the way Jesus became hungry, began looking for something to eat, and came across a fig tree in full leaf. At this time of year, a fig tree wouldn't have yet borne mature figs, but edible buds should have already been visible. Finding nothing but leaves on the tree and no fruit, Jesus did something that seems to bother some commentators: He cursed the fig tree.

I have no problem with this, primarily because it's in the Bible. I also have no problem with it because I believe the fig tree is symbolic of Israel and the temple at the time. Remember, Jesus was on His way to the temple, where they were worshipping God but didn't even recognize that the promised Messiah was in their midst. Their worship and religion were promising but barren. So Jesus cursed the fig tree and cleansed the temple of the money changers because neither were producing fruit.

Note that the money changing in the temple was occurring in the only area where the Gentiles could come to find God. Mark records that Jesus said, "Is it not written, 'My house will be called a house of prayer for all nations?' But you have made it a den of thieves!" (v. 17). The gospel was for all men, but those leading in temple worship were hindering the Gentiles from coming to faith.

Would people call the church you attend a house of prayer? Are you known for your prayer ministry? If people had a prayer request or were seeking God, would they think of you first? Or would they come and find that the stuff of religion has blocked their way to the cross? Would they come looking for evidence of the Christian life but find instead a barren, formal, dead religion—one that *says* it has the key to abundant life but produces nothing consistent with it?

I've dealt with a lot of people over the years who have used Jesus' cleansing of the temple to forbid selling books or products in the church foyer after a concert or a guest speaker's appearance. But let's be biblical here. That's not the point. The point is, the money changers were keeping the Gentiles from a place where they could find faith. Jesus was dealing with hypocrisy, not record sales. Don't misuse this passage to support legalistic preferences.

Jesus and His disciples left the temple and headed back to Bethany. But the next morning on their way back to Jerusalem, they passed the cursed fig tree, and Peter was surprised that the curse had worked. Jesus replied by saying:

> Have faith in God. I assure you: If anyone says to this mountain, "Be lifted up and thrown into the sea," and does not doubt in his heart, but believes that what he says will happen, it will be done for him. Therefore, I tell you, all the things you pray and ask for—believe that you have received them, and you will have them. And whenever you stand praying, if you have anything against anyone, forgive him, so that

> your Father in heaven will also forgive you your
> wrongdoing. But if you don't forgive, neither
> will your Father in heaven forgive your wrong-
> doing. (Mark 11:22–26)

Notice that Jesus didn't even respond to Peter's statement about the fig tree being withered. Instead He jumped immediately to the subject of faith. "Have faith in God" (v. 22). This phrase literally means to be constantly trusting in God. Praying in faith does not mean you'll get whatever you want. A segment of the Christian community teaches health, wealth, and prosperity, which verges on communicating that God is our servant, not our Sovereign. They teach that we can make demands on God. I don't believe this sort of praying is biblical or faith-based. Praying by faith must be consistent with the will and Word of God. As Thomas Watson said, "Prayer is the key of heaven; faith is the hand that turns it."

In the days ahead Peter and the other disciples would face many obstacles. The opposition would be great. They would need to remember these truths as God called them to take the gospel to the Gentiles and stand boldly against a dead religion.

HOW MOUNTAINS MOVE

Mountains are often seen in Scripture as something insurmountable or impossible, a difficult task. From the disciples' vantage point, Jesus could have been looking toward the temple mount when He spoke about lifting up mountains and throwing them into the sea. On a clear day they could have seen the

Dead Sea from this position. He wanted the disciples to learn that faith must not be in systems, formulas, or religion, but in God and God alone.

Augustine wrote, "What is faith, unless it is to believe what you do not see?" I might not see a physical mountain being moved, but that's not the point. The point is that power is available to us by faith in God through prayer. Nothing is impossible with God. Jesus taught His disciples that the key to prayer is not faith in faith, but faith in God. God is the object of our faith. We overcome by faith in God, not in our own abilities. Faith is never any greater than its object.

Think about it. How can I say, "I have faith to believe God for salvation," if I don't have enough faith to believe that He cares about the opportunities and obstacles I face while on earth? Thomas Adams wrote, "It is the office of faith to believe what we do not see, and it shall be the reward of faith to see what we do believe."[1]

Manley Beasley was the greatest man of faith I ever met. He was a walking miracle and knew how to trust God in ways I can't even begin to grasp. Often he would ask people as he met them, "What are you trusting God for today?" Our faith in God to move the mountains in our lives is an active, daily faith.

To have mountain-moving faith, we must focus on God, not on the mountain. J. C. P. Cockerton said, "Faith does not grow by being pulled up by the roots time and again to see how it is getting on. Faith grows when we look steadily towards God for the supply of all our needs and concentrate on him. There is little point in becoming engrossed with our faith as if that were the thing we believed in!" Jesus didn't tell us to try to work up faith. He told us to focus on the One who is our source and strength. Once our focus is set, then "if anyone says to this mountain, 'Be lifted up and thrown into the sea,' and does not doubt in his heart, but believes that what he says will happen, it will be done for him" (v. 23).

"Therefore, I tell you, all the things you pray and ask for—believe that you have received them, and you will have them" (v. 24). This is faith's confession and God's command to trust Him. Many of us pray with a "hope so" attitude rather than a "know so" attitude. I love what Ron Dunn said when I heard him preach on this passage: "I consider the problem, but I don't take the problem into consideration." The problem is not our priority; having faith in God is our priority. The mountain is not the issue; God is the issue.

OUR FAITH GROWS AS IT IS STRETCHED. THE BIGGER OUR UNDERSTANDING OF GOD, THE BIGGER OUR FAITH.

If we're honest, we'll admit that most of our praying is filled with doubting. We are hesitant to ask, for fear we might fail—or worse, for fear that God might not be able to answer. Just do what God says. Let Jesus stretch your faith and increase your prayer life. We wonder, Am I insane to ask God for this? What will people think if I tell them I'm believing God for it? Is it in the will of God? Ask this instead: Is it in line with the Word of God? Is the Holy Spirit bearing witness with my spirit that I can ask this? Then ask, and stop doubting. You're not asking on the basis of *your* authority but on His.

I can imagine where you're probably being tripped up right now. You want to believe God, but can you really expect Him to do the impossible? Yes you can, and yes He can.

> But let him ask in faith without doubting. For the doubter is like the surging sea, driven and tossed by the wind. (James 1:6)

> Now this is the confidence we have before Him: whenever we ask anything according to His will, He hears us. And if we know that He hears whatever we ask, we know that we have what we have asked Him for. (1 John 5:14–15)

One reason we don't believe God with mountain-moving faith is that we are often too logical. We can't easily move from the five senses to the unseen. We have been conditioned all our lives to see, feel, touch, smell, and taste. So by nature we need to see it to believe it. That's not faith, however. Just as you never advance in school until you pass the tests, you can't advance in the school of prayer until you're willing for your faith to be tested.

Jesus calls us to exercise our faith. We *have* faith by *having* faith. Our faith grows as it is stretched. The bigger our understanding of God, the bigger our faith. The late Vance Havner was fond of saying, "Nothing is more disastrous than to study faith, analyze faith, make noble resolves of faith, but never actually to make the leap of faith."

In studying this passage I ran across a thought from Charles Kingsley which stirred me to think about the powerful truth that we can pray for the impossible. "What an awful weapon prayer is! Mark 11:24 saved me from madness in my twelve months' sorrows; and it is so simple and so wide—wide as eternity, simple as light, true as God Himself; and yet it is just the last text of Scripture which is talked of, or preached on, or used."[2]

Allen Atkins is a friend of mine who pastors in Alabama. I asked him to share a story about a recent mission trip that will encourage you to pray with faith and not doubt.

> In March 2008 our church was scheduled to go on a mission trip to a small village in Romania. The purpose of our trip was to plant a new Baptist church in a village that had no evangelical church. Several months had been spent in preparation for this trip. We knew that all the roads in and around the village were dirt roads and that everyone who planned to attend the worship services at night would have to walk. So we planned to walk house-to-house during the day to visit, encourage, pray, and share Christ with the people. Therefore, we needed good weather. The problem is, in Romania in the month of March, we could have either pleasant weather or very nasty weather. And every piece of information we gathered indicated the weather was going to be nasty, with

heavy showers and even snowstorms forecast for the week of our trip.

Several weeks before our departure, our team began to gather weekly for prayer. The weather, of course, was one of the main things we prayed about. During this time the Lord directed me to that familiar passage in James 5. One night during our prayer time, I read verses 16–18. I told the group, "I believe God wants us to believe and have faith that He can hold off the rain for the days we are in the village. If He can hold off the rain for three and a half years, as He did during Elijah's time, I believe He can hold it off for three days." So that's what we began to pray.

As the weeks went by, our faith and fervency increased. One night during our prayer time, one of the men said, "I'm going to pray that it rains up until the day we arrive, that it doesn't rain while we are there, and that it starts raining again when we leave so the people will know that it's God." Every report continued to show heavy rain and the possibility of snow for the week of our trip. We were determined, however, that we would not let the reports shake our faith. We even printed out the dismal weather reports so we would have future testimony to the power of God.

The week of our mission trip arrived, and as we approached the village, we could tell it had been raining for many days. Water was standing in the fields. The roads were so muddy that they were almost impassable. The skies were dark all around the village, which is set against a mountain range, and black clouds were coming over the mountains. Four of us went to the top of a hill that overlooked the village. We continued to pray in faith that it would not rain. We have photographs that show the village surrounded by dark clouds with an opening of bright sunshine directly overhead. For the three days we ministered in the village, it did not rain!

We were able to visit in the homes. Individuals and families were able to walk to the services at night. By the third night, we had 145 people in attendance. We know of around seventy-five people who prayed to receive Christ, and we gave a brand new Romanian language Bible to everyone who came.

On the final night as we were boarding the bus to leave the community building where we met for worship, a heavy rain began to fall. But for three days, God had shown Himself faithful to a group of believers from Alabama who dared to believe that God is who He says He is and that He can do what He says He will do. Today there is a new church in the village of Chilia, Romania, that is a testimony to the faithfulness and power of a God who loves it when His people begin to pray and believe Him and His Word.

God always has the last word. The mountains quake at His presence. He will split the Mount of Olives when He returns. So whatever your mountain, take it to God by faith and believe Him as you never have before. Jesus is not telling you to try to move literal mountains. He is telling you to believe God when facing difficulties and impossibilities. It is my opinion that the disciples remembered this lesson as they gathered to pray in the Upper Room, waiting for the coming Holy Spirit.

> **WHATEVER YOUR MOUNTAIN, TAKE IT TO GOD BY FAITH AND BELIEVE HIM AS YOU NEVER HAVE BEFORE.**

But don't stop here.

OH, AND ONE MORE THING

There is a condition that must be met for our mountain-moving prayers of faith. We would like to talk about this and forget the condition, but here it is. Jesus continues in verse 25, "And whenever you stand praying, if you have anything against anyone, forgive him, so that your Father in heaven will also forgive you your wrongdoing. But if you don't forgive, neither will your Father in heaven forgive your wrongdoing" (vv. 25–26).

Charles Spurgeon wrote, "You are nothing better than deceitful hypocrites if you harbor in your minds a single unforgiving thought. You can't be saved unless you are forgiving; if we do not choose to forgive, we choose to be damned."

Let's be clear here. If God is not answering your prayers, you need to check your heart for any unforgiveness. Is there anyone you can't or won't forgive? Is there any hurt you can't stop talking about? Are there any unresolved conflicts in your life? If so, you are limiting what God can do *in* you, *through* you, and *for* you because of unforgiveness. Some folks would honestly rather miss a blessing than get right with God.

The word "forgive" here is present tense in the original language. It means to be always forgiving. It's a lifestyle, not just something you do at youth camp or some annual event. It means to remit and send away that which could get in our hearts and pull us down. You cannot separate prayer and forgiveness.

This hearkens back to Jay Strack's illustration at the beginning of this chapter. No forgiveness, no power. Jesus Himself presses the point; therefore, we are unable to justify any seemingly insignificant areas of unforgiveness. It's "anything against anyone," He says.

Naturally some folks are easier to forgive than others. But I learned a long time ago that it doesn't take a brain the size of a peanut to hold a grudge. *Dogs* forgive and forget better than humans do. I'm not saying it's easy, but I am saying it's right. You and I can't ask God for mercy if we are unmerciful. We can't ask Him to forgive our sins if we don't forgive those who sin against us.

Back in 1995 I went through a difficult time as a pastor. I had three staff members leave within months of each other. One of them, however, refused to ride off gently into the night. Despite the fact that he had basically quit doing his job nine month's before officially resigning, we graciously continued to keep him on staff and to pay his full salary until he could find another place of service. By the time he finally left, I was frustrated, and he (by all accounts) remained extremely bitter.

A few years after he left, I was sitting in my office on a Sunday morning about to preach on forgiveness. Suddenly the Holy Spirit convicted me about this matter. Although in my heart I felt I had done all I could do, I sat down and wrote him an e-mail asking if we could get together and talk at the upcoming Southern Baptist Convention. He sent a curt, cold response, "If you need it, we can get together, but I don't need it."

At first I got ticked off. But soon I realized that I had done what God had told me to do. It was now the responsibility of this brother to do the right thing. So I laid it before the Lord. To this day I have run into his family members who are also in the ministry, and they barely speak to me. I could go into a hundred things we did for this staff member to try to give him an honorable exit, but he just didn't get it. He has chosen the path of unforgiveness. I can't fix him or the situation; I can only handle my part. As best I know how, I've laid this at the altar and have no ill feelings toward him.

I certainly don't share this as a means to further inflame the situation but only to show how unforgiveness can eat away at us until we don't even realize we've lost the ability to forgive as

Christ forgave us. Our vertical relationship with God is damaged if our horizontal relationships with others are not where they should be.

When I was in youth ministry, I was let go from a church I was serving. The best way I know to describe it is, the pastor and I just got off track. I did some things that hurt him deeply and said things I shouldn't have said. Forget who was right or wrong, I *knew* I was wrong.

One day I was attending a conference in Houston, Texas, and saw my former pastor and his wife coming down the sidewalk. We had lunch together, and I asked him to forgive me for things I had done wrong. He has preached for me in both of the churches I have pastored, and I consider him a dear friend today. A relationship was restored and a friendship actually deepened because we both understood the importance of forgiveness.

I've seen this work with husbands and wives, parents and children, and employees and employers. I've seen it happen in revival services. If you want to see your church set free, get over the stuff that binds you.

WHERE GRUDGES GO TO DIE

I once served the First Baptist Church of Trivial Pursuit. It seemed as though every week people were singing B. J. Thomas's "Another Somebody Done Somebody Wrong Song." I heard complaints about every former pastor, living and dead. Finally I got up one Sunday and announced the theme for the coming year, to be put on our mail-outs, our letterhead, and everywhere else we could find. Our theme would be, "GET OVER IT!"

I then began to run through the laundry list of things I had heard from unforgiving lips. "Brother So-and-So didn't come to see me in the hospital, and I've just never gotten over that." "Brother So-and-So said something to my kids in Sunday school, and I just can't forgive him." "Sister So-and-So hurt my feelings, and I'll never go back to the choir." I finally asked one lady in particular, "When was Brother So-and-So here?" She said sharply with a tone that could cut steel, "1948 to 1952!" I said, "Ma'am, that was more than twenty-five years ago, and he's been dead for ten of them." She responded, "But you don't know how much he hurt me." Honestly, I could trace every cantankerous deacon's meeting, every ugly business meeting, and our total lack of witness in that community to one thing: an unwillingness to forgive.

Phillips translates this verse, "You must forgive any grudge you are holding against anyone else." The spirit of this passage is so obvious that you don't need to be a Greek scholar to understand it. If you're running down someone, holding a grudge, or even if there is something so irritating about a person that you can't stand to be on the same planet with them, you'd better forgive if you want God to forgive you.

John Bisagno, in his book *The Secret of Positive Praying*, tells the story of an old television show in the 1950s where one of the main characters complained that his friend was always slapping him on the back, but he was getting tired of it. He decided to get even by strapping a piece of dynamite to his back. The next time this friend slapped him on the back, he was going to blow his hand off!

Bisagno commented on that show by saying, "In holding a grudge of unforgiveness against someone else, we don't do anything but blow ourselves up with our own inability to receive forgiveness. That dynamite blows both ways, and that unforgiveness flows both ways as well. So when we judge others, we must remember that we're not God. Let God judge. Forgive, and we will be forgiven."[3]

Anything that builds a wall between you and someone else is in essence building a wall between you and God. Some people think they only have to forgive if the other person is truly sorry about what they've done. Sometimes we want those who are seeking our forgiveness to beg and grovel before us. That's not the spirit of forgiveness; that's the spirit of holding a grudge.

If our Lord could hang on the cross and say, "Father forgive them," who are you and I to hold a grudge against anyone—about anything? When you and I learn to forgive, we will no longer use past hurts against the person who committed them. We'll move forward and not talk about it any longer. We need to forgive to the same extent and with the same spirit that Jesus forgave us.

John Owen, the Puritan writer, said, "Our forgiving of others will not procure forgiveness for ourselves; but our not forgiving others proves that we ourselves are not forgiven." When you pray, have faith . . . but don't forget to forgive if you are expecting anything from God.

CHAPTER 7

WARFARE PRAYING

Ephesians 6

We must wrestle earnestly in prayer, like men contending with a deadly enemy for life.
—J. C. Ryle

With every prayer and request, pray at all times in the Spirit, and stay alert in this, with all perseverance and intercession for all the saints.
—Ephesians 6:18

THE *U.S. Marine Corps Book of Strategy* states, "Positions are seldom lost because they have been destroyed, but almost invariably because the leader has decided in his own mind that the position cannot be held."[1] The Christian life is a war. If we don't understand this, we will live defeated lives. Daily we are involved in a battle, a spiritual conflict. The church is not a cruise ship; it's a battleship. Too many believers are in a spiritual ditch by default because they've never prepared themselves for the long road of discipleship.

I minored in history in college, and I was always particularly interested in studying the Civil War. That war led to more casualties than any other in the history of our country. Hundreds of thousands were killed or maimed for life. The battles were blood baths where brother fought against brother. There have been many reasons given for the War Between the States, from slavery to states' rights. The bottom line is: war is inevitable when there is a conflict between two opposed wills, philosophies, or worldviews. The friction can take many different forms, but it will ultimately move from friction to a fight.

In this chapter I want us to look at prayer as it relates to spiritual warfare. John MacArthur writes that spiritual warfare is "a war of universal proportions pitting God and His truth against Satan and his lies. It's a battle of wills between God and Satan. It's a cosmic conflict that involves God and the highest creature He ever made and it filters down to every human being. Satan and his army of demons are fighting Christ, His holy angels, the nation of Israel and believers. The battle lines are clearly drawn."[2]

In the Christian life we are in a war with the world, the flesh, and the devil. We wrestle. It's hand-to-hand combat. Satan hates everything we love. He fights on every front imaginable. The battle is most often in the mind, which is why Paul calls us to renew our minds. As students of the Scripture and servants of the King, we shouldn't be surprised that we are in a war.

But it's not just any war.

The Marine manual also states, "All actions in war take place in an atmosphere of uncertainty—the *fog of war*. Uncertainty pervades battle in the form of unknowns about the enemy, about the environment, and even about the friendly situation. While we try to reduce these unknowns by gathering information, we must realize we cannot eliminate them. The very nature of war makes absolute certainty impossible."[3]

While the statement above may be true from a human perspective on war, it is not true about spiritual warfare. We are *not* ignorant of Satan's devices. He is crafty, subtle, and persistent. He is seeking whom he may devour. But we have been equipped by the Spirit and through the Word to be overcomers. We have not been left alone to figure out the strategies of the enemy. We have been given clear instructions on how to prepare.

I often tell people that Satan is predictable. He has used the same schemes and methods since the Garden of Eden. His very names, outlined for us in Scripture, reveal his character and his methods. And if we as believers understand this, we can be prepared for battle. The devil is like a riverboat gambler—he always plays his trump card too early—which is not very surprising when you consider that patience and self-control are among the fruit of the Spirit. It is obvious, therefore, that Satan would be impatient and unable to control himself. So when he plays his trump card, we don't need to panic. When his assaults come, we can detect his tactics and respond correctly. We can know what we're dealing with and how to face the battle.

Basically, we have been called to war on the floor. The battle is on our knees. We have a Lord who said, "All authority has been given to Me in heaven and on earth" (Matt. 28:18)—not to Satan or demons or governments or circumstances. All authority—ultimate authority—is God's. Yet most of our prayers in times of battle sound like our God is struggling to maintain control of the palace. We must understand that we can walk in victory.

THE WINNING HAND

Much of our defeat as believers can be directly tied to prayerlessness, often attributed to a lack of faith or disbelief in the promises of God. Just get a concordance and do a search of the phrase "in Christ," and see if you are thinking and praying in accordance with who you are in Him.

Vance Havner adeptly identified the problem of prayerlessness when he wrote, "The church is not developing her recruits into disciplined soldiers. We are fighting the greatest battle of all time with the most untrained army on earth. If strict discipline is necessary in art and athletics, how can we expect to be advanced Christians and stay in kindergarten?"[4] Too much of our praying and resisting looks like a soldier waving an empty scabbard bereft of its sword. Prayer meetings have become a thing of the past. According to some studies, the average Christian prays less than five minutes a day. Most of the members of our churches are AWOL when it comes to prayer. We don't believe in the power of prayer because if we did, our attendance would reflect it.

Does your praying in times of conflict, stress, and adversity reflect these Scriptural promises and principles?

> Who can separate us from the love of Christ? Can affliction or anguish or persecution or famine or nakedness or sword? . . . No, in all these things we are more than victorious through Him who loved us. (Rom. 8:35, 37)

> Therefore, my dear brothers, be steadfast, immovable, always excelling in the Lord's work, knowing that your labor in the Lord is not in vain. (1 Cor. 15:58)

> But thanks be to God, who always puts us on display in Christ, and spreads through us in every place the scent of knowing Him. (2 Cor. 2:14)

> Because whatever has been born of God conquers the world. This is the victory that has conquered the world: our faith. (1 John 5:4)

The old song says, "From victory unto victory, His army shall he lead, till every foe is vanquished and Christ is Lord indeed." Most praying I hear sounds like we're trying to move from defeat to victory instead of from victory to victory. Victorious, believing prayer does not rest on what I have done—or even on what I say—but on what *He* has done and what *He* has said. We have victory because He is the victor.

> **BELIEVING PRAYER DOES NOT REST ON WHAT I HAVE DONE BUT ON WHAT HE HAS DONE.**

Finally, be strengthened by the Lord and by his vast strength. Put on the full armor of God so that you can stand against the tactics of the Devil. For our battle is not against flesh and blood, but against the rulers, against the authorities, against the world powers of this darkness, against the spiritual forces of evil in the heavens. This is why you must take up the full armor of God, so that you may be able to resist in the evil day, and having prepared everything, to take your stand.

Stand, therefore, with truth like a belt around your waist, righteousness like armor on your chest, and your feet sandaled with readiness for the gospel of peace. In every situation take the shield of faith, and with it you will be able to extinguish the flaming arrows of the evil one. Take the helmet of salvation, and the sword of the Spirit, which is God's word.

With every prayer and request, pray at all times in the Spirit, and stay alert in this, with all perseverance and intercession for all the saints. Pray also for me, that the message may be given to me when I open my mouth to make known with boldness the mystery of the gospel. (Eph. 6:10–19)

Paul describes in this passage all the weapons needed for warfare. He gives us our spiritual armor for warfare on our knees. Our problem is not a lack of funds, inadequate facilities, or a need for organizational restructuring. Our problem is a lack of understanding of prayer. Satan will let you witness if you just don't pray because he knows that prayer moves the heart of God, that prayer is the realm in which God works behind the scenes. Satan opposes Godward prayer, and he opposes you personally.

One of the keys to Sherwood's success has been her prayer ministry. We bathe our projects, goals, and strategies in prayer. In relation to the films developed by Sherwood Pictures, we pray over the story idea, script writing, casting, filming, editing, and the film's release. Often I call our church to pray that we might stay humble and focused on the main thing when we are in this arena. Why? Because we are invading enemy territory. Hollywood is a dark place. For too long Christians have shunned Hollywood and not confronted the problem. We've whined when we should have been praying. We've hidden our lights under a bushel. We've cursed the darkness instead of turning on the light. Without prayer, we are walking into enemy territory without our armor.

When we released our second movie, *Facing the Giants*, the MPAA gave it a PG rating for "football violence." Immediately we were inundated with calls and requests for interviews. We did more than three hundred interviews with secular and Christian media about the film and, believe me, we had to be prayed up when answering live questions on national television.

One of the lines from *Facing the Giants* referred to fear colliding with faith. Often throughout the film, Coach Grant Taylor's fears intersected his faith, and he was forced with the decision to trust God and believe His Word or allow his fears to control his life. Isn't that what happens when we pray? Our faith and fear are on a collision course, and we are faced with some questions: Will our faith overrule our fear? Will the promises of God in His Word be more real to us than what we fear?

When we released the third film, *Fireproof*, we caught the attention of Hollywood and the press when the movie opened on 839 screens (the Hollywood average is around 2,500–3,000 screens), and finished #4 in total box office receipts and #2 in per-screen average on opening weekend. We bathed that movie in prayer. If you watch the film, you'll notice a prayer coordinator listed in the credits. We especially focused on praying for our own marriages.

God opened doors again with this movie that only He could have opened. We've been asked to explain why a movie, largely ignored by Hollywood, did so well and made it in the top five on opening weekend. Our answer has been simple, "We bathed it in prayer, and we know you can't predict what God can do." Whatever God has done through Sherwood Pictures must be attributed to surrendering to the Lord and appealing to Him to do beyond what we could ask or imagine.

I repeatedly warn our church to stay prayed up. Making a movie that deals with the crisis of today's troubled marriages in America and calls people to believe God for the impossible will stir up our enemy. As a result, marriages in our church were under attack. Some attacks were blatant, but most were subtle. The enemy has a variety of methods, but it was predictable that he would attack in the area where we were trying to send a clear message.

Warren Wiersbe is a dear friend and wise counselor. He and I talk a couple of times a month. We catch up on family and talk about ministry, but I also seek his advice. I can remember two distinct times when we have seen God do something incredible that he has said to me, "You'd better get ready. The devil is going to be angry. You're going to be in increasing warfare." Any time you put yourself on the front lines, you are going to be a target.

In August 2008 more than three thousand people gathered at the historic Fox Theater in Atlanta to screen *Fireproof* at an event sponsored by The WinShape Foundation. It was an incredible night. The fellowship was sweet and the room was electric. It was a night to remember. I woke up the next day, however, to a phone call from a staff member telling me that someone had tried to firebomb our church the previous night. By the grace of God, their scheme didn't work. But it reminded me that we needed to have our guard up and our armor on. In the midst of our celebration, the enemy was at work. We needed the startling reminder to keep our knees to the ground and our eyes fixed on Christ.

We need to understand the priority of prayer. We are fighting a spiritual battle for the heart of the church and the souls of men. The enemy will not go quietly into the night. He is a defeated foe, but he is still dangerous.

PREPARED FOR PRAYER

Paul gives us instructions in Ephesians 6 regarding our adversary, our armor, and our assignment. After describing the armor, however, he concludes with a thought that might look out of place to the casual observer. "With every prayer and request, pray at all times in the Spirit, and stay alert in this, with all perseverance and intercession for all the saints. Pray also for me, that the message may be given to me when I open my mouth to make known with boldness the mystery of the gospel" (vv. 18–19). Yes, we are given the armor so we can stand and pray. Warfare is prayer, and prayer is warfare.

We know this, yet it seems we have resigned ourselves to defeat as the norm.

- *We waste our time fighting on the wrong battlefield.* We think our enemy is the culture, Hollywood, or Washington, D.C., but our enemy is not flesh and blood.

- *We show up at the wrong war.* We can be sidetracked while fighting for "a good cause" and not fighting for the cause of Christ.
- *We major on the minors.* We quibble about what kind of body position is appropriate for prayer, or whether or not we should have our quiet time in the morning or the evening.
- *We treat spiritual things in a casual manner.* We believe there are things we can handle by ourselves, though Jesus clearly said, "Apart from me, you can do nothing."
- *We limit our prayers to selfish asking.* Our prayers are largely about my wants, my needs, my desires. Try praying for a week without praying about anything personal, and see if it changes the way you pray.

Warfare is not really in the physical realm; it's in the spiritual realm. The focus of our praying, both individually and corporately, must be taking back what the enemy has stolen. He is a thief, liar, and destroyer.

I have to say that praying is the hardest thing I do. It's easier to prepare a sermon than to pray. It's easier to write a book than to pray. It's easier to write a book on prayer than to pray. It's easier to witness than to pray. It's easier to picket and write Congress than to pray for those in authority. It's easier to talk about people I don't like than to pray for them. Prayer is difficult because there is so much at stake in the spiritual realm.

Paul says, "We win the battle in prayer!" This is not the same as saying, "We will just let God do it." Some people have confused prayer with passivity. Not so. It means we need to get our priorities straight. The average church spends more time on buildings, budgets, campaigns, and calendars than on prayer and intercession. They have a committee on committees, but no prayer ministry. They have fellowships at the drop of a hat but won't drop to their knees in worship for extended prayer. No prayer yields no power.

Paul tells us in Ephesians that we are to put on the armor with all prayer. We are to deal with the enemy through prayer. Prayer is our secret weapon. It is more powerful than any military tactic, weaponry, or explosive man has ever created.

BATTLE ON

If you are honest, you will probably have to admit that your prayer life is not where it should be. I do not say this to make you feel guilty. I say this because admission leads to confession. I have to admit I'm prayerless before I'll do anything to change my prayerless condition. Advancement in prayer begins with an admission of my need to pray.

Our adversary, the devil, looks for ways to manipulate and outmaneuver us. Sometimes he is so subtle that, if we're not praying, we don't even see him coming. He works on us to compromise and waste our lives. Before we know it, we've wasted a day, then a week, a year, and maybe most of our lives.

The only way to have victory is through Christ. We cannot fight "against the rulers, against the authorities, against the world powers of this darkness, against the spiritual forces of evil in the heavens" (v. 12) by trying harder in our flesh. Our puny human efforts will fail. Our responsibility and calling is to stand and pray. Remember this: careful organizing, sincerity, or trying to do your best without prayerful agonizing is a disaster.

The late A. W. Tozer wrote about the warfare of the Spirit:

> It is the Spirit of Christ in us that will draw Satan's fire. The people of the world will not much care what we believe and they will stare vacantly at our religious forms, but there is one thing they will never forgive us—the presence of God's Spirit in our hearts. They may not know the cause of that strange feeling of antagonism which rises within them, but it will be nonetheless real and dangerous. Satan will never cease to make war on the Man-child, and the soul in which dwells the Spirit of Christ will continue to be the target of his attacks.[5]

If we are who we're supposed to be, Satan will oppose us. He doesn't bother those saints who don't bother him. He will leave the prayerless believer alone. But when we are actively engaged with God in prayer, we become noticed in dark, devilish places. This is why Paul would tell us it is important to know your enemy, to be aware of your adversary, to "take your stand." The very statement implies opposition, someone trying to push us off the field of play or the field of battle. Someone is trying to undercut us. We must take our stand—and not just stand, but stand firm.

To stand is to hold your ground. It is the opposite of retreat. The Scriptures are clear regarding our position in Christ and how we are to practically live out our understanding of that position. To be in a praying position and to boldly pray, we must know who we are in Christ or else we will pray like a pauper and not a soldier. We stand in the victory already won by Christ at the cross. We pray from a position of victory.

I love the hymn "A Mighty Fortress Is Our God" by the great theologian Martin Luther:

> And though this world, with devils filled, should threaten to undo us, / We will not fear, for God hath willed His truth to triumph through us: / The Prince of Darkness grim, we tremble not for him; / His rage we can endure, for lo, his doom is sure, / One little word shall fell him.

Because of Christ, the devil has been stripped of all his weapons. Jesus has overcome all we have to fear—death, hell, and the grave. We are dead in Christ, and Satan can't put fear into a person who has already died to himself. Jesus has also openly disgraced him. "He erased the certificate of debt, with its obligations, that was against us and opposed to us, and has taken it out of the way by nailing it to the cross. He disarmed the rulers and authorities and disgraced them publicly; He triumphed over them by Him" (Col. 2:14–15).

There is no victory in self-help methods, greater will-power, or positive thinking. These concepts may sell in the marketplace, but they have no value in the heavenlies. We are to stand on the ground that Christ has won the battle for us. We are commanded to "be strengthened by the Lord" and to "put on the full armor of God." It's not either/or—it's both/and. Our strength is not in our flesh; it's in the Lord. But at the same time, we have to stand firm.

FULLY ARMORED

As I was looking through commentaries regarding this passage, it struck me that Paul had preceded these instructions on warfare with instructions on a godly marriage. There is no victory in the home or in the church without a battle. Warfare praying deals with the practical things of life. It is not reserved for only major frontal attacks. It is designed to be the pattern of our praying. We stand, we claim the promises, and we ask in believing prayer as the norm, not the exception.

One of the first books I ever read on spiritual warfare was *The Christian in Complete Armour* by William Gurnall. This is not a bedside book

> **WE STAND IN THE VICTORY ALREADY WON BY CHRIST AT THE CROSS. WE PRAY FROM A POSITION OF VICTORY.**

for a casual reader. It is more than a thousand pages long and biblically deals with how Satan works against the saints, how God has equipped believers with His armor, and how to use His weapons. Gurnall makes clear that we are at war with the devil. This is not a causal, infrequent skirmish but an all-out war. It's a book worth adding to your library.

Please note the number of times you read the word "against" in these verses from Ephesians 6: "against the tactics of the Devil," "not against flesh and blood," "against the rulers, against the authorities, against the world powers of this darkness," and so on. Many commentators agree this listing of various forces reveals to us various powers with different functions. There is someone who is against us. He has all kinds of weapons at his disposal. We can't be ignorant of these devices and schemes.

Other biblical accounts prove the validity of Paul's admonition. We read the stories of Eve, Achan, and David, and find a consistent theme: "I saw," "I coveted," and "I took." With Elijah, the attack was discouragement. With Simon Peter, it was denial. With others, it was unbelief. With some, the enemy tried to hinder the work of God. Paul talked about Satan hindering him. Satan's attacks are designed to destroy, distract, frustrate, discourage, and defeat us. He tempts us to doubt God's Word. Paul wants us to know our enemy.

Prior to these words on spiritual warfare, Paul commanded the Ephesians to be "filled with the Spirit" (5:18). The filling of the Spirit is not a way to escape trials and temptations; it is the power necessary to face them. If we try to win the battle in the strength of our flesh, we are going to get shot down by a flaming arrow.

Paul baptizes the armor of the Roman soldier and gives it spiritual application. He could also be going back in his mind to Isaiah 59:14–21 where we see a picture of God Himself dressed in battle array, fighting for His people. God fought for Israel, and He fights for us. He supplies all that is necessary to win.

The Lord will finally bring judgment on His enemies at the Second Coming of Christ. Right now, He has equipped us with the necessary armor to stand against our enemies.

The armor that God supplies is *His* armor. We don't make or manufacture this armor. We can't buy it at the local Christian bookstore. No, we apply the armor that is provided by God. The coming, conquering King is giving us armor that allows us to overcome. We appropriate what He has given us in order to find victory. I know people who daily begin their prayer time by praying through the armor, piece by piece, knowing they are going into battle that day.

The armor allows us to stand against the onslaughts and to attack with the offensive weapon of the sword of the Spirit. Paul reminds us in 2 Corinthians 10 that our war is not against the flesh, and our weapons are not carnal or fleshly. We don't engage in warfare praying by trying to reason out what we need to do or what Satan is trying to do. We stand, fight, and pray with the mind-set of bringing every thought captive to the obedience of Christ.

H. A. Ironside wrote:

> Every one of us who has put our trust in the Lord Jesus Christ has been made the righteousness of God in Him. We stand before God in Christ, but we do not put this on ourselves. God has clothed us. But when it comes to the panoply for conflict, we need to put on each separate piece of armor in order to withstand in

the evil days when the hosts of hell are pressing upon our souls and it seems as though we
would be borne down and defeated. We are not
to turn our backs and flee from the foe. We are
not to act on the presumption that "he who
fights and runs away may live to fight another
day," but we are to face the foe, for there is no
armor for the back. If we turn our backs, if we
retreat, we but expose ourselves to the fiery
darts of the wicked one, but as we face the foe
unflinchingly in the power of the finished work
of Calvary we shall be able to stand.[6]

Stand in who you are in Christ. Stand on what God says
in His Word. Stand in the full armor of God. Take the provisions given to you. Take the resources at your disposal and stand
praying.

The hardest victory to win is the victory over self. The
thought that "I can handle this" or "I can try harder or do better"
is disastrous in spiritual warfare. We are called to be an army of
prayer warriors, not armchair saints. Alan Redpath says, "There
is no winning without warfare; there is no opportunity without
opposition; there is no victory without vigilance."

This is no time to sit on Jordan's stormy banks and cast a
wishful eye. There are battles to fight, Jerichos to confront, and
issues that cannot be ignored. To rest in Christ does not mean
we've been released from battle. The kind of rest that requires
no fighting is for the next life, not this one.

It is impossible to be a growing, praying Christian and not fight. We are in a war with sin, self, and Satan. J. I. Packer said, "Regeneration has made our hearts a battlefield." There is a volume of truth in that statement. The day you came to Christ, you became an enemy of Satan.

CLOSING IN PRAYER

Neither time nor space allows me to discuss all the aspects of our armor. There are better and broader works than this one that can help you understand all the armor you have available to you. Gurnall's book, along with Warren Wiersbe's *The Strategy of Satan*, would be valuable resources to your study. I will only mention the importance of the sword of the Spirit. The Word and prayer go together. You can't be effective if you have one without the other. Power to pray and knowledge of the Scriptures are inseparable.

In the 1970s I heard a youth speaker explain to students how they could use the Word in their prayer life. He said, "First of all, hold the Word of God up to the Lord. The Bible is our prayer book, our book of promises, our basis for praying with authority." Then he told them to hold the Word of God up against the devil because the devil can't stand the truth (see Ps. 60:12; Isa. 54:17; 1 John 3:8). We are to remind him that he is a defeated foe. Finally he said, "Learn to pray with the sword. You do that by praying the Word back to the Father and quoting the Word back to the devil."

Paul in no way suggested that prayer is in addition to the armor. He clearly suggests that it is *part of* the armor. We arm ourselves so we can pray. One writer calls prayer "the atmosphere in which all our fighting occurs." Warren Wiersbe writes, "We put on the armor by means of prayer, and we pray by means of the Holy Spirit."[7]

You can't wield a powerful, effective sword or stand firm without prayer. One of the old hymns, "Stand Up, Stand Up for Jesus," says, "Each piece put on with prayer."

- Pray as you put on "truth like a belt around your waist."
- Pray as you put on "righteousness like armor on your chest."
- Pray as your "feet [are] sandaled with readiness for the gospel of peace."
- Pray as you "take the shield of faith."
- Pray as you put on "the helmet of salvation."
- Pray as you use "the sword of the Spirit, which is God's word."

There is no compartmentalized approach to warfare praying and standing firm; this is the comprehensive plan of God. If you don't pray through each element of the armor, none of them will work as they should. We communicate with the King through prayer. We communicate with the Captain of the Lord of Hosts through prayer. We approach the throne through prayer. Prayer is the key to appropriating all we have in Christ.

Warfare praying is a daily reminder of our absolute dependence on God for strength, victory, assurance, peace, and power. Spurgeon said that conflict is the principle feature of the Christian life this side of heaven. That being true, if we are going to face the conflict, we have to face it on our knees.

Nothing is discussed more and practiced less than prayer. Prayer that costs nothing is worth nothing; it is simply the by-product of a cheap Christianity. To win the day, we must pray. E. M. Bounds wrote, "Other duties become pressing and absorbing and crowd out prayer. 'Choked to death' would be the coroner's verdict in many cases of dead praying if an inquest could be secured on this dire, spiritual calamity." We are powerless because we are prayerless. It's not that we don't have the right equipment; it is that we fail to appropriate it.

Prayer is the key to victory. If we do not pray, we will fall to temptation and sin. If we do pray, we will flee from such things. Andrew Murray warned, "Beware in your prayer above everything of limiting God, not only by unbelief but by fancying that you know what He can do." How do we know what He can do? How do we know what to pray? By studying the Word. The sword has to be sharpened to be effective. We must be students of the Word so we can renew our minds, restore our souls, and pray with confidence.

Paul instructed that we are to pray "with every prayer and request" (v. 18). What kinds of prayers is he referring to here? Both general and specific, big and small. As I said before, if it's big enough to worry about, then it's certainly big enough to pray about. The stronger we become in the Word, the more powerful we will become in prayer. Turn your Bible into a prayer book.

Also, don't skip past the word "every"—as in "every prayer and request." If you do, you might run headlong into the enemy.

This word implies that we are to exhaust all our resources in prayer; we are to persist in praying. Paul said something similar to the Thessalonians when he wrote in his first letter to them, "Pray constantly" (1 Thess. 5:17). In the New Testament we find the early church facing persecution and constantly going to God in prayer for more boldness.

If we have any desire to move from victim to victor, we must learn this principle. The fight is great and persistent. If we don't pray, we will give up or be shot down. We will shrink in the hour of battle, let our fellow soldiers down, surrender because of unbelief, or grow weary in well-doing. We can't afford to let these things happen. We are in a war, and we are to stand in order to *with*stand the onslaughts of the enemy.

The one thing the disciples asked Jesus to teach them was how to pray. We know that Jesus had an active ministry on earth, but obviously He set aside time to pray. Prayer was a priority for our Lord. If our Lord needed prayer to sustain Him, how much more do we need it?

As you read Paul's epistles, it is clear that we are to pray about everything that touches our lives. We pray because we are commanded to pray. We pray because of the example set by our Lord. We are called to pray without ceasing, though obviously we can't walk around with our eyes closed or stay in the prayer closet all day long. It is imperative to have a time and place of prayer, but we must also learn to pray on the go. There is a spirit of prayer that must always be prevalent in the prayer warrior.

James Philip writes, "If we are right people, then we will pray always, and if we are not, we cannot and we will not; even if we were on our knees all day long, we would not pray as God means us to pray. It is not how we pray, and what we pray, but what we are when we pray, that is decisive. Our life is our prayer. And if our life is not right neither will our prayer be right, however earnestly we may stir ourselves in prayer."[8]

The key is what Paul talked about throughout Ephesians: all that we have in Christ motivates us to live a life pleasing to God. It's not enough to pray longer prayers. Warfare praying is the result of a believer who understands discipline, the Word, and the control of the Spirit. Only then do we have a life that can pray.

Having been to Israel several times, I am always fascinated by the Wailing Wall. To see hundreds of sincere people standing before the wall, putting their prayers in the cracks of its surface is indeed a moving picture. But is this the way God works? I believe that prayer—warfare prayer in particular—is about having a *life* of prayer, a life lived all day long with a God-consciousness, a constant awareness of His presence, and a constant dependence on His promises.

THIS IS WAR

I certainly don't understand everything there is to know about prayer. I'm reminded of the words of Thomas Edison spoken nearly a hundred years ago, "We don't know the millionth part of one percent about anything. We don't know what water is. We don't know what light is. We don't know what gravitation is. We don't know what electricity is. We don't know what heat is. We have a lot of hypotheses about these things, but that is all. But we do not let our ignorance about these things deprive us of their use."[9]

Prayer is an active word. In the New Testament it often means to wish forward or to desire onward. In prayer we are in a war that demands us to desire onward. We are not content with things as they are. We are boldly approaching the throne of grace. We are standing firm when opposed by the enemy. We are marching onward and upward when it would be easier to retreat. The times of testing reveal where our faith rests and what we really believe about God.

Make sure your praying is in the Spirit—not your will but His. The Spirit helps us in our weakness (see Rom. 8:26). The Spirit of God bears witness with the Word of God and gives us what we need in the moment. With this in mind our prayer life should be specific so that we can stand firm and remain steadfast. I don't know all there is to know about warfare, but I do know that God has called us to pray and to put on the armor. That's all I really need to know. The doing is my responsibility.

In the 1990s I was faced with a very difficult task that every pastor dreads. I had brought the whole team together to voice their opinions on calling a new staff member. By all outward appearances he looked as though he would be a great fit, but we quickly discovered he was being divisive by playing the staff against one another, playing members against me, and so on. The rest of the staff came to me and said, "Either he has to leave, or we will leave. He's of the devil."

(Just a tip here: Satan sometimes doesn't fight churches; he joins them. When you see divisive, mean-spirited people in the church, you'd better step up your praying before the devil gets an upper hand in your fellowship.)

Back to the story. This staff member was disloyal. We caught him lying and misrepresenting me to the staff on numerous occasions. When all the facts were in, our deacons voted unanimously to let him go. He was given a generous severance package and left quickly. But within hours he was lying about the whole process. He told members he had been left destitute, and soon people were taking up money for him. He started telling godless and demonic stories about me, the staff, and others. People were furious.

All of this happened on a Thursday. The following Sunday, we were scheduled to host an evangelist for a one-day crusade. I was tempted to call him and cancel because I was embarrassed that he would walk into such a situation. I was in the middle of a crisis that demanded more than I could do on my own.

We started praying. People who knew the facts started seeking God. We prayed as a staff. We asked God to reveal the deception and protect His church. The forty-eight hours after the firing were some of the longest in my ministry.

When the evangelist arrived, I felt obligated to tell him about the situation. I told him that I didn't know what would happen on Sunday. He related to me that on his flight to Albany, the Spirit of God spoke to his heart and asked him, "How many folks will you believe Me for in this meeting? How many will you pray for to be saved?" He said he asked God for fifty.

My first thought was, "Oh, no, that's not going to happen." But then something stirred in me, reminding me that God does

His best work in the darkest hour. We approached Sunday with a certainty that God would do something to show Himself as Lord in those services.

At the end of the day, we baptized more than forty people and had more than fifty come to Christ. Although the devil had his moments—some still found reason to criticize—Jesus ultimately won the day.

As Winston Churchill said, "Never give in. Never. Never. Never." The battle is raging, the enemy is fierce, and the way ahead is treacherous. Nevertheless, as Paul writes, "In all these things we are more than victorious through Him who loved us" (Rom. 8:37).

CHAPTER 8

PRAYING FOR YOUR CHILDREN
Deuteronomy 6

To pray effectively we must want what God
wants—that and that only is to pray in the will
of God.
—A. W. Tozer

I have no greater joy than this: to hear that my
children are walking in the truth.
—3 John 4

I NEED PRAYER WARRIORS, so I try to surround myself with people who boldly approach the throne of grace. Two of my closest friends in the world are Roger and Linda Breland. Roger was the founder of TRUTH, one of the pioneer contemporary Christian groups that toured America and the world for more than thirty years. Roger will tell you that Linda is a true prayer warrior. She's one of those folks who knows how to get before God and to intercede for others. She's currently in charge of the prayer ministry at the University of Mobile and is one of the first people I write, e-mail, or call when my wife, Terri, or I need prayer support. She knows how to agonize and believe God in prayer. I asked her to share some thoughts on praying as a parent.

> After recently rereading numerous pages of my journals from twenty years ago, I stand amazed at how desperately I prayed for my three sons and husband and how faithfully God moved mountains in answering my cries to Him.
>
> Some of my life's verses are "Faithful is He who calls you, and He also will bring it to pass" (1 Thess. 5:24) and "Great is Thy faithfulness" (Lam. 3:23). God is faithful! My journals of answered prayers are a powerful, ongoing testimony of the faithfulness of God.
>
> Some of these intercessions for my children included prayers about which colleges they would attend, the mates they would marry,

and the careers they would pursue, but most of all I prayed for their personal spiritual walks with the Lord. Often the Lord would call me to fast and pray in hard situations. Many times I prayed against strongholds I recognized in their lives. Most of the time the Lord would give me a specific verse to pray and hold on to—a promise to write their names on. I learned that my peace came from trusting the Lord, never in watching the circumstances. Isaiah 26:3 says, "The steadfast of mind Thou wilt keep in perfect peace, because he trusts in Thee."

Often the Lord would lovingly remind me to quit trying to control and direct their lives and release them into His strong arms so He could work out His plan. At certain stages I literally felt that I was raising these sons on my knees in my prayer closet. God hemmed me in and pressed me to Himself—it was the only way I could make it. And I found in Him everything I needed: His help, peace, strength, and wisdom. I clung to Jeremiah 33:3—"Call to Me and I will answer you, and I will tell you great and mighty things, which you do not know."

Today I'm still praying for these three sons and three beautiful daughters-in-law and thirteen precious grandchildren. Let me encourage you to make prayer a priority, no matter what season of life you are in with your children! It will be worth your time, energy, and sacrifice. Do not let the enemy use busyness, worldliness, and prayerlessness against your families. Prayer is simply intimate communion with our Father. Intercession is asking for those we are praying for to have a meeting with God. We are a "go-between," asking for a breakthrough between heaven and earth.

I recently studied and meditated on many verses concerning prayer. As I opened my journal, I began to write down these questions that I sensed the Spirit asking me. When will you quit talking about prayer and just pray? When will you throw out routine prayer and cry out in desperate prayer? When will you believe Me for everything you are asking Me for? When will you be devoted to prayer, keeping alert in it and not losing heart but persevering? Will you keep on asking without ceasing and pray about everything? Will you pray My way with forgiveness and humility from an obedient heart? Will you pray in My Name and for My glory only and for My will to be done? Will you pray in agreement with others with boldness and confidence? Could you not watch with Me for at least one hour?

Catherine Booth of the Salvation Army is said to have prayed, "Oh, God, I will not stand before Thee without my children." Each of her children came to Christ and became a preacher. Jonathan Edwards claimed from God that none of his seed would be lost. He claimed the salvation of his children, grandchildren, and great-grandchildren. I read somewhere that a study was done of Edward's descendants, and not one was found who was not a believer.

I've read that Mrs. A. J. Gordon, wife of the founder of Gordon College and mother of five, believed that God would never let a child of believing parents be lost. All of her children were saved. I heard the story of a man who had ten children. On his deathbed he was smiling as he entered his last moments of life. A friend at the bedside asked, "How can you smile when not one of your children is saved?" The elder said, "I settled that long ago. I brought them up as God commanded me, and every one of them will be in. They're a strong-headed group, but God will lead them." All of them came to Christ.

WHAT EVERY CHILD NEEDS

Nothing brings more happiness, fear, and anxiety to our hearts than our kids. They can be our greatest joy and our most devastating heartbreak. Having earlier served in youth ministry for fifteen years, I have seen the effects prodigal children have on families. Too often their parents fret, worry, bail out, and make excuses without seeking God in believing prayer.

I've never met anyone with perfect kids. I've met some grandparents who thought they had perfect grandchildren, but then I met the nursery workers who took care of them and learned they weren't so perfect. I read a humorous story in a 1980 *Reader's Digest* written by Jean McMahon from Dyer, Indiana. She said, "Attending church in Kentucky, we watched an especially verbal and boisterous child being hurried out, slung under his irate father's arm. No one in the congregation so much as raised an eyebrow—until the child captured everyone's attention by crying out in a charming Southern accent, "Y'all pray for me now!"

When you pray for your kids, I think it is important to remember a few things:

1) God gave His children, Adam and Eve, the perfect environment and they blew it. You won't have perfect kids. They don't have perfect parents.

2) God desires the best for your kids and for you. He sent His Son and has given you the Holy Spirit so that His life can be lived out through your life.

3) We are stewards of the lives entrusted to us, but there is a point when children are responsible for their own actions.

4) Our God can give us the wisdom we need to know how to respond to our children. He's given us His Word and the wisdom of other believers.

5) Our God has the power to set the captives free. We need to believe Him when we pray for our prodigals to come home.

Unfortunately we've been deceived into believing it's the responsibility of the government or the school system to train our children. Thus, it's easy to think we can dump all responsibility on the church as well. But the church can't resurrect what the home puts to death. Parents have the first and foremost responsibility in training children.

Therefore, they should also prioritize the privilege of covering their children in prayer.

I love this quote from the late A. C. Dixon: "When we rely upon organization, we get what organization can do; when we rely upon education, we get what education can do; when we rely upon eloquence, we get what eloquence can do, and so on. Nor am I disposed to undervalue any of these things in their proper place, but when we rely upon prayer, we get what God can do."[1]

We pray for God to bless our kids, protect our kids, and help our kids in school. But is that enough? If we are going to change the culture and raise godly children, we need to learn how to genuinely, desperately pray for them. Studies show that up to 92 percent of teenagers today are not affiliated with any church, cult group, or religious organization. That means we've lost this generation. It is also said that of the eight percent who attend church, over ninety percent of them will drop out of the church after high school. The problem is epidemic. We need a spiritual solution through intercessory prayer that lays hold of God on behalf of our kids. This is no time to limit family prayers to "bless our kids" as we say grace over the meal. The enemy is out to destroy your kids, your home, and the next generation.

We have a thirty-foot banner hanging on the wall in our church atrium that says, "Whoever wants the next generation the most will get them." We want to be used of God to raise children and students in the nurture and admonition of the Lord. That's why we've built the sports park I mentioned, complete with baseball, softball, soccer, and flag football fields, tennis courts, a fishing pond, an equestrian center, and more in order to reach families with children. But if that's all we do, then we have failed. We must pray to the Lord of the harvest that we can be used by Him to touch them and reach them for Christ. We must partner with parents in showing kids a better way than the one portrayed in most movies, music, and media.

THE ENEMY IS OUT TO DESTROY YOUR KIDS, YOUR HOME, AND THE NEXT GENERATION.

We have prayed over the fields at the sports park countless times. We've prayed for the families we would one day reach. We've prayed for children to come to Christ because of the influence of Christian coaches. We've written hundreds of prayer cards, as I said, that will be encased in the base of the cross that stands at the center of that property.

Prayer is not optional. It's not a last resort, for use only when we are in a crisis. We should consistently and purposefully pray for our children. I would encourage you to gather with other parents to pray for each other's kids, and be sure to partner with single parents as well.

What's the greatest thing you can ever do for your kids? Teach them to have good manners? Boy, some need that. If you go to a restaurant these days, you wonder if some kids were raised in a barn. Teach them to be polite to senior adults and to those of the opposite sex? That's a good thing. Provide a good education? We all want our kids to get the best education possible. Teach them to manage money? Yes, they should be taught to be good stewards of the things God gives them.

All these are good, but the greatest thing you can ever do for your kids is to pray for them. Think about it. You can't be with them 24/7. Sooner or later they leave the safety of the home and head out to school, to work, on a date, or off to college. You can't protect them from everything and everybody. There will come a time when their friends will have as much influence on them as you do. The only thing you can do that will follow them for life is to bathe them in prayer.

In my library I have more than a hundred books on parenting and the family. I can't find one that deals specifically with praying for children. Several deal with having a family altar. Others deal with making sure they're in church. But specific instructions on praying for children are nowhere to be found. If we want to be effective parents and give our kids the best possible shot at being all God designed them to be, we need to get before our heavenly Father on their behalf.

WHAT IT LOOKS LIKE

The best place to start praying for our children is the Word of God. "A house is built by wisdom, and it is established by understanding; by knowledge the rooms are filled with every precious and beautiful treasure" (Prov. 24:3–4). The writer of

Proverbs talks about building a house with wisdom. He's not talking about being an expert or memorizing Dr. Spock. He's not telling you to be prepared to be a guidance counselor for kids. He is discussing how to build a family on biblical principles. Remember this: prayer is a foundational principle of the Word of God. You can't read the Word without knowing that prayer is essential.

Before we can truly pray for our children as we should, we must do some self-examination. First of all, do we want our kids to just be good, or do we want them to be godly? Unfortunately I've met parents and grandparents who didn't want their kids to be "too spiritual." They didn't want to raise missionaries and preachers; they just wanted kids that wouldn't embarrass them. That's not good enough. That's not a motive God will bless.

Are you committed to being an intercessor for your kids? Isaiah understood the lack of intercessors. "The LORD saw that there was no justice, and He was offended. He saw that there was no man—He was amazed that there was no one interceding" (Isa. 59:15–16). How tragic. No one—not one—to intercede. I wonder how many kids have lived without ever hearing their parents pray?

I can tell you the only times I ever heard my dad pray was over a meal. For years I was the designated "pray-er" in our family. I don't ever recall walking into the house late at night after curfew and finding my dad on his knees pleading for me.

I have a friend who is a fellow pastor. He told me the story of how he came in late one night, trying to tiptoe past his parents' bedroom. He could see his dad on his knees, praying and crying out to God for his son. That rattled my friend's cage and has impacted him for the rest of his life. I know a lot of moms who are prayer warriors, but we desperately need praying dads.

The psalmist said, "I give myself to prayer" (109:4 NKJV). Are you giving yourself to prayer? Do you only pray for your kids when they're in trouble? Or do you pray that they will have wisdom to avoid trouble? Do you ever pray Scripture for your kids? Have you ever thought about praying the prayers of Paul and personalizing them for your children? It's a good place to start.

I would also suggest that the words of Moses in Deuteronomy about parents' responsibility to teach their children is a reminder that God holds us accountable to pour the things of God into the lives of our kids. For intercession to be effective, it must be a way of life, not a hit-or-miss proposition. Prayer is the key that unlocks heaven's storehouse of blessings. Before you can pray for others, prepare yourself. You will be praying against the world, the flesh, and the devil that all seek to undermine and destroy your home. If we are going to get before God on behalf of our children, we need to make sure our own hearts are right.

> How can a young man keep his way pure? By keeping Your word. I have sought You with all my heart; don't let me wander from Your commands. I have treasured Your word in my heart so that I may not sin against you.
> (Ps. 119:9–11)

> If we confess our sins, He is faithful and righteous to forgive us our sins and to cleanse us from all unrighteousness. (1 John 1:9)

We must purge our hearts of any thought or attitude that would hinder our praying with authority. At the same time, we must admit that we need the Holy Spirit to help us know how to pray. We can pray selfishly when it comes to our kids. We can want for them what seems best to us. We need to get to the point where we can pray, "Not my will, but Yours be done." We need to give them back to God since they are first and foremost His children. We are just the stewards, but we need to be good managers of our stewardship.

We need to consciously die to our own ideas of what is best for our kids. We can get in our minds what career path we think they should be on, what college they should attend (surely God wants them to go to my alma mater), who they should marry, and so on. We can try to "fix" our kids, making them into our image rather than the image of Christ. Honestly there are times when we don't pray; rather we make suggestions to God on our knees because our motives are mixed. It is at this point that we must pray according to His will. Our Father does know best.

As you pray for your kids, praise God in advance for what He is doing and what He will do in their lives. Pray in faith. As fallen men and women, we are sinful by nature. We were born into sin. But if I, as an imperfect dad, want my kids to be blessed and be a blessing, how much more does my heavenly Father want to pour Himself out on their lives?

KEEPING IT REAL

Here are some practical tips when praying for your kids:

1) *Pray according to the Word* (1 John 5:14–15). God's will never contradicts God's Word.

2) *Pray as a matter of lifestyle* (Luke 18:1). Don't pray only when your kids are in trouble. Pray while they're in the womb and throughout the rest of their lives.

3) *Approach the throne of grace boldly* (Heb. 4:16). Pray as a matter of faith and claim the victory. Some people pray like they're scared of God. Others pray as if they're approaching the bench of a vengeful judge. You are talking to your heavenly Father who gave the best He had—His Son. The veil has been torn, so go before the throne and cast all your anxieties upon Him because He cares for you.

4) *Pray believing that God hears your prayer* (1 Pet. 3:12). Pray on the authority of God's Word.

5) *Recognize that standing in the gap for your children puts you on the front lines of spiritual warfare* (Eph. 6:12). Ask God to show you specific things you need to pray about, to make you sensitive to areas where your children are vulnerable.

Think about all the areas where your kids need your bold intercession. Kids can be cruel to other kids. Peer pressure can be unbearable. Put-downs and sarcasm are the order of the day. You need to pray that God will give your kids stamina to stand against peer pressure, as well as the wisdom to know when someone is trying to deceive them.

I often tell people that I learned a lot just keeping my mouth shut in the car. Our girls would talk about what happened at school, things that were worrying them, who was drinking or sleeping around or lying to their parents. Rather than react, I just listened, while pretending to listen to the radio. Then I knew how Terri and I should pray for them and for their peers. I tell schoolteachers to just walk the halls and listen to the conversations at the lockers to know how to pray for their students.

IF YOU WANT TO KNOW HOW TO PRAY, GET INVOLVED, AND YOU'LL GET MORE THAN YOU CAN SAY GRACE OVER.

When our older daughter, Erin, was a cheerleader and our younger daughter, Hayley, was playing basketball, I would sit in the stands right behind the team and watch the game. But I was also observing and listening to the students' conversations. I was determined to be involved as much as possible. I wasn't perfect, but I was there. I never missed a home game while Erin was cheering or while Hayley was playing basketball. I was busy, but not too busy for my family. If you want to know how to pray, get involved, and you'll get more than you can say grace over.

One reason the home in America is in trouble is because of absentee dads. Dads aren't paying attention. In too many homes, the mom is the spiritual leader. Dr. W. B. Riley said:

> The longer I live I am more persuaded that the
> average husband is making a mistake at the

very point where he has supposed himself to be
the most successful. He can delve sixteen hours
a day and coin a mint of money, and construct
a beautiful house, and hedge it about by a great
and attractive lawn, and multiply his automo-
biles, and increase the number of servants, and
every bit of it will be accepted by the woman
who is his mate as her natural right. And then
he has no time left to be gentle, and tender,
and gracious, and complimentary as in old days
of wooing and poverty. Thus she and the children are almost certain to conclude that the
affections are gone![2]

Let's admit that none of us have perfect children, that we
aren't perfect parents. The Scriptures are full of godly, sincere
people whose children failed or broke their heart. There are
also countless stories of families that failed to take their faith
seriously.

- Adam and Eve's first son was the first murderer.
- Jacob's sons sold their brother Joseph into slavery.
- The children of Israel who were delivered from Egypt
  failed to lead their children into the Promised Land and
  set a bad example for their kids. They looked at circumstances rather than listening to God. They weren't willing to take God at His Word, and consequently they
  spent forty years in the wilderness.

- Eli's sons were priests, but they were worthless men.
- After Joshua, a generation arose that rebelled against God's will.
- David's son Absalom rebelled against him.

Let me make this clear: just because you love your kids and want God's best for them doesn't mean your kids will be perfect. I know many, many godly parents who have some sorry kids. You can't allow yourself to be beaten up by Satan, the accuser of the brethren. Kids make choices. They are responsible for their actions. But you and I still have a responsibility to pray and believe God for our kids.

Let me also say that kids can't forever blame their parents who don't walk with God. "That's just the way I was raised" won't stand up as an excuse at the judgment seat. If your parents don't walk with God, you don't have to follow the same pattern. After fifteen years in youth ministry and nearly twenty-five as a pastor, I can tell you that some of the greatest young people I've ever known have come from families where the parents weren't saved or committed. The key is not environment as much as attitude.

As you pray, remember every child is unique. God said to Jeremiah, "I chose you before I formed you in the womb; I set you apart before you were born" (1:5). Samuel was a child of promise to a praying woman. John the Baptist was born to be the forerunner for Christ. Obviously not all children are born to be prophets or priests. But the truth is, God knows us. God forms us. God gives us our personality. God determines the number of our days. Therefore, we need to get in tune with what God had in mind when He entrusted us with these children.

Our two daughters are great friends, but they are as different as night and day. One wants to be on stage, front and center. She's an actress and loves to perform, and you could see it from her earliest days. The other one prefers to be behind the scenes. She would rather make things happen and manage situations than be out front. We have always prayed for them in different ways. If no two snowflakes are alike, then no two children are alike either. Every birth gives us an opportunity to seek the Lord. There is no cookie-cutter formula for successful child rearing. Each child is a unique gift from God.

I heard one researcher has concluded that at birth there are 4,500 predispositions in a child. Besides physical differences, many variations of personality and ability exist. Talk about something that will drive you to prayer! Think about how you pray for a daughter differently than you do for a son, or how you pray for an introvert as opposed to praying for an extrovert. Match your specific praying to your unique child.

WALK THIS WAY

The catch-all verse for the average parent is Proverbs 22:6. "Teach a youth about the way he should go; even when he is old he will not depart from it." That verse could be translated, "Modify the will of a child, the way he is bent, and when he becomes a teenager, that pattern will stay with him," or "Adapt the training of your child so that it is in keeping with his God-given characteristics and tendencies; when he comes to maturity, he will not depart from the training he has received." I believe (though many may disagree with me) that this verse is a principle, not a promise. I know a godly man and woman whose son committed suicide. I know others whose children have walked away from God. Is it the parents' fault? I don't think so. They prayed and pled with God for their kids, but their kids made bad choices. It can be destructive to make a principle into a promise.

Chuck Swindoll said:

> The wise parent realizes the sovereign God of heaven has given the gift of children. He has planned and arranged and prescribed with certain attributes, abilities, personalities, and physical appearances. By study and observation, this parent gets to know the child God has given him. He spends time in prayer asking for wisdom. He spends time watching, talking with, and listening to that precious child, not just when he is little but all through the years the child is at home. The parent actually becomes a student of the child because the parent knows this child has certain established bents.

The word "way" in Proverbs 22:6 means a mode, manner, or course of life. Psalm 11:2 uses the term to describe an archer bending his bow before he lets the arrow fly to the target. Psalm 127:3–5 uses arrows as a picture of children. Children are like arrows. They need to be aimed in the right direction. We need to pray that we put the right amount of tension on the bow as we guide them toward the target. Under God's guidance we need to train our children according to His "way."

The way of your child is different from your own. This means parents have to adapt their training and parenting to each individual child. Again, your child has a certain bent or personality. They are uniquely different.

> For it was You who created my inward parts;
> You knit me together in my mother's womb.
> I will praise you, because I have been remark-
> ably and wonderfully made. Your works are
> wonderful, and I know this very well. My bones
> were not hidden from You when I was made
> in secret, when I was formed in the depths of
> the earth. Your eyes saw me when I was form-
> less; all my days were written in Your book and
> planned before a single one of them began.
> (Psalm 139:13–16)

God oversees the entire pre-birth development. This is why abortion is a sin against God. It is an act of taking a life that has been ordained by Him. He watches over the children in the womb. He has watched over the abortion of tens of millions of innocent children who had no say in their lives.

Could it be that God has a book on every person? He forms our bodies. Some He makes short; others He makes tall. Some are high-strung; some are laid back. Some are very emotional while others are almost stoic. Some are athletic and some are artistic. But all are designed by God. Make your intercession proactive, not reactive. Pray early and often. Be on the offensive, not on the defensive.

PRAYER GUIDES

With all of these things in mind that we've explored in this chapter, I want to suggest some principles I've learned and gleaned along the way in regard to praying for your children.

1) *Pray they will know Christ early in life* (Ps. 63:1; Isa. 45:8; 2 Tim. 3:15). Twice a year we dedicate parents and babies in our church. Often the front of the church is covered up with parents and kids standing before the congregation. One thing I always pray is that these children will come to know Christ at an early age. I pray they will be like Timothy, coming to Christ early because of the loving influence of family. I long for them to find Christ as a child so they will be spared the scars of sin that deepen as we get older.

I remember when our oldest daughter came to Christ. Having raised her in a pastor's home, I wanted to be careful that I didn't push her. One night after church we were sitting in the living room. I knew that the key was to see if she understood the concept of sin. We talked for a few moments, as we had at other times, then I tried to send her on to bed and told her we would talk later. She said, "But Daddy, if I died tonight I would go to hell." I asked her how she knew that. She said, "Because I know I'm a sinner. I've sinned against God." She realized, even at that young age, that her sin was not in lying to us or not respecting our authority, but it was ultimately and foremost against a holy God. That night she prayed and came to Christ.

Pray for your children's salvation, but don't pressure them to be saved. Alan Stewart, one of my pastor friends, shares the story of his daughter's salvation. She didn't become a Christian until she was a teen, though she was raised in the church by godly parents. Read Alan's story and see how he balanced authoritative teaching with sensitivity to the Spirit in the life of his daughter.

During our September 2002 church revival, I was kneeling at the altar praying when my son Seth, who was five at the time, came and knelt beside me. He was clearly under conviction and understood his need for forgiveness and salvation. Jeanne and I were taken by surprise because we had obviously missed the signs the Lord was speaking to our son. As wonderful a moment as this was for our family, there was the looming concern over our daughter Sierra who was two years older than Seth. Seth had always been a black and white thinker, but Sierra was more analytical in her thoughts. Everything has to fit before she will accept or trust anything.

With the passing of years, there were moments when Jeanne and I could see the weight of conviction on her life. We attempted to "strike while the iron was hot" by sitting down with her and walking through the plan of salvation. She always said she understood but was just not ready to make a decision. With the frustration mounting, I knew if I did not back away and trust her to the Lord, she would either harden her will or she would make a decision under pretense just to please me. As much as I wanted Sierra to be saved, I wanted her, as I say to my church family, "to know that you Know that you KNOW you are saved."

Backing away and trusting her heart to the Lord was the hardest thing in the world to do as a parent. I had read and preached on all the passages about getting your children to Jesus, and yet my own daughter was not saved. From the time my son Seth was baptized, I baptized eighty-five children and youth, and still my own daughter was lost. As excited as I was for those families, each child I took beneath the water only reminded me of my own failure. In my own imagination I thought that when Sierra saw many of her friends being baptized, she would surely feel compelled to follow suit. That never happened.

Sierra was now turning thirteen, and my greatest fears were becoming reality. I knew all of the statistics about children being saved in their youth and how difficult it became as they grew into adulthood. I could sense the window of opportunity closing quickly. We had dedicated her as a baby to the Lord, and she had been in church from the moment we took her in her carrier at one week old. She had already heard more sermons than the average church member. My church family knew the pressure of this burden was overwhelming, and many committed to pray with us over Sierra's life.

It was at this point I remembered a story I had read years ago about a father praying for his daughter. The father had taken his family into the mountains to camp for the weekend. When they arrived at the campsite, they found the grounds littered with debris from the previous campers. As they began to clean up the site, they discovered a Bible that had been left behind in the debris. The father opened the Bible searching for a name, but found none. Flipping through the Bible, he discovered notes from sermons and devotion times in the Bible that gave the appearance of a young boy's handwriting. That night the father prayed that the Lord would send into his young daughter's life a boy with a heart for God just like the boy who owned this Bible.

Years passed. His daughter moved away to college. There she met a wonderful young man and asked if she could bring him home to meet her parents. When the young man came to visit, he was examining the books in the library of her father, when his eyes were startled at what he beheld. It was that old Bible from the camp-site. The young man asked the father where he got this Bible, and the father went through the long story about finding it in the trash left at a campsite in the mountains, but there was no name inside that he was able to return it to. The young man looked at the father and said, "You need to look no further. The Bible belongs to me!" The Lord had answered his prayer!

This father had prayed specifically and strategically, and I knew this is what we had to do as well. We began praying for the Lord to lead people into Sierra's life that she trusted and would be willing to open up to. At summer youth camp, our student minister's sister, Jenny Robertson, would be that person. Jenny saw the conviction on Sierra's face after the evening devotion and began to share Christ with her. Jenny said nothing that we had not already said, but perhaps a fresh voice along with the timing of the Lord had put all the pieces together in Sierra's mind. She called me just after midnight, and I will never forget the tenderness and peacefulness in her voice when she said, "Daddy, I just got saved." The Lord had now completed the circle of my family in salvation.

A youth camp leader asked me if, as a preacher, it bothered me that I was not the one who got to lead my daughter to Christ. I answered, "If your house were on fire with your children still inside, would it bother you that I ran inside and pulled them from the fire rather than you?" I learned again the valuable lesson that power still belongs to the Lord, and salvation is a sovereign act of His graciousness.

The prophet said it best in Jeremiah 33:3, "Call unto Me, and I will answer thee, and show thee great and mighty things, which thou knowest not."

This prayer for the salvation of your children should also include a prayer that they will walk in the fullness of the Spirit and have a desire for the Word of God. Pray they will have an appetite for the things of God and will realize that in God's Word are truths to believe, promises to claim, and commands to obey. Pray they will love God with all their heart, soul, mind, and strength.

2) *Pray they will have a hatred for sin* (Ps. 97:10; Rom. 16:19; 1 Thess. 5:6). We live in a world that teaches us to

excuse sin. We are so worried about being weird that we aren't holy. We worry more about our kids being accepted in school than being accepted in the Beloved. I don't want them to hate sin if they get caught; I want them to hate sin, period! I want them to understand the price people pay when they willingly sin against God.

Your kids face daily pressure to be like the world. We must pray that while they are *in* the world, they are not *of* the world. Pray that as they face temptations, peer pressure, and attacks from the enemy, they will be transformed daily by the renewing of their minds.

3) *Pray they will get caught whenever they sin* (Ps. 119:71). I prayed that no matter what our girls did, they would get caught quickly. Whether it was disobeying a rule or trying to see what they could get away with, I wanted them to get caught. I prayed that Terri and I would not be the dumb parents we see so often. I see kids who dress and act in provocative ways while their parents seem to be clueless. I wonder when I see some girls, "Don't the dads remember what they thought about girls who dressed provocatively when they were teenagers?"

I am grieved to see how naïve or willfully ignorant some parents are. They don't know what their kids watch on TV. They don't know who they're getting text messages from. They have no clue what their Facebook or MySpace page looks like. Why? The kids have their own TV and computer in their rooms, and parents never check up on them. I know parents that don't use parental controls on their TVs and computers. They are asking for trouble and heartache.

Several years ago our youth minister had some concerned parents in his office. They thought their son might be looking at porn on the Internet. The youth minister asked, "Where's the computer?" They said it was in his room, and he spent a lot of time in his room with the door locked. The youth minister told them to take the computer out of his room and put it where it could be seen, restrict his use, and get a filter. Their response? "But that would be an invasion of his privacy!" No, that's protecting him.

If you are praying for your kids to get caught, be prepared. They may embarrass you. But it is worth losing a little pride rather than living with a broken heart. Better that someone in the community think less of you than for them to comfort you because you didn't stop your kids before it was too late.

WE WORRY MORE ABOUT OUR KIDS BEING ACCEPTED IN SCHOOL THAN BEING ACCEPTED IN THE BELOVED.

4) *Pray they will be protected from evil influences in their lives* (Prov. 3:3; John 17:15). Satan wants to get a stronghold in the lives of your kids in order to pull them down. Pray over them that God will protect them from those who try to put them into bondage.

During our annual ReFRESH™ Conference at Sherwood in 2008, Tom Elliff spoke one evening on the curse of words. He talked about some of the things people can say that are evil and put us in bondage for years. It could be a passing, cutting remark or a hateful insult. Either way, if we hold onto these words and begin to believe them about ourselves, they can ultimately have more authority in our lives than the true Word of God. We saw hundreds of people freed from the curse of words, walking in freedom and in the power of God's truth.

Also pray that your children will not buy into the lie that fame, fortune, power, and pleasure are the ultimate things that matter. Pray they will not develop faulty values or a watered down worldview of success and life. Ask God to protect them from being won over by the false thinking and deception of finding self-worth in how they look, what they wear, or what others think of them.

The world is setting traps for your kids. Pray they will not fall into temptation and will take every thought captive to the obedience of Christ. Pray that your children will confess quickly and repent deeply of wrong choices. Pray they learn to say a firm "no" when tempted to compromise. Pray that they have clear discernment.

5) *Pray they will have a responsible attitude in all their interpersonal relationships* (Prov. 1:10–11; 1 Cor. 15:33). Pray for your kids as they make decisions regarding their friends and dating relationships. Don't push them to have a boyfriend or girlfriend. Too many parents are ruining their kids by talking about boyfriends and girlfriends when they are preschoolers. They aren't ready for this until they're at least mid- to late-teens. They may look physically mature for their age, but they aren't emotionally mature to date until they're in the late high school years.

Do you know the kids your children are hanging out with? Are you absolutely sure your kids are really with the people they say they're with? This isn't an issue of not trusting your kids. Unfortunately our culture drives a wedge between parents and children, teaching them it's OK to mislead as long as they don't get caught.

You and I both know that the need for acceptance is a major issue with kids. They need to know they are loved just the way they are. Pray that as parents you can be the role models they need and can give them everything they need to be emotionally and mentally secure in who they are. Pray that others will partner with you in encouraging them to be all God designed them to be.

Pray that your children will be kind (1 Thess. 5:15) and generous (1 Tim. 6:18–19) like the Macedonians who "gave themselves" (1 Cor. 8:5). Pray they maintain humility (Phil. 2:1–5; Titus 3:2) and a servant's heart (Eph. 6:7). Pray they are pure in heart (Ps. 51:10; Matt. 5:8). Pray for your kids to have courage to do the right thing (Deut. 31:6) with self-discipline (Prov. 1:3). Pray they will persevere and finish well (Heb. 12:1).

6) *Pray they will respect those in authority over them* (Rom. 13:1; 1 Pet. 2:17). One of my favorite scenes in *Facing the Giants* confronts this very issue. Following football practice one afternoon, Coach Grant Taylor sees one of his players, Matt Prater, treating his father with great disrespect. When Coach Taylor confronts Matt about the issue, the teen blows off the issue without another thought. Later in the movie, however, we see God work in Matt's life. He asks Coach Taylor to take him to his dad's office so he can apologize in person. Matt's father, as well as his coworkers, are dumbfounded.

One of the most disheartening characteristics of the current generation is their complete disregard for authority. Children and teens often run their homes, ordering their parents around like hired help. But respect for authority is more often caught than taught. If you don't respect your boss, a government authority, or the church leadership, don't expect your kids to respect you. Good leaders are first and foremost good followers. If your children surrender to the authority of Christ in their lives, they can be servant leaders who impact the world for Christ.

Pray your kids will learn the biblical meaning of words like accountability, integrity, and honesty. Pray they will learn to listen to the right people, remembering that life is determined by the books they read, the choices they make, and the people they spend time with.

Kids today are taught to be sarcastic, rebellious, and cynical. Pray they will have the mind of Christ and the fruit of the Spirit evident in their lives. I often tell parents that if you teach your children to respect authority and exhibit the character of Christ, there is no limit to their potential. Why? Because they will stand out in a crowd of compromisers.

7) *Pray they will be kept from the wrong mate and save themselves for the right one* (2 Cor. 6:14–17). We live in a society that seeks to redefine marriage, but God's Word has not changed on the subject. Marriage is a covenant. Jill Briscoe, in her excellent book *Fight for the Family*, uses Nehemiah as an example of the boundaries necessary to protect our homes. The Bible has set the clear bounds for marriage and family. These boundaries are not to limit us but to protect us for our good. She writes:

The ruined boundaries have been buried under so much rubble that confusion lies within the minds of many. "What does a real marriage consist of anyway?" inquire puzzled, mixed-up teenagers. "Are you telling us," they ask, "that two people living in hatred and hostility within the walls of their legal contract—proud possessors of a marriage certificate—are any more married than two lovers who genuinely care for each other yet do not possess that magic piece of paper?" Our children are listening to those free spirits who, eager to cast off all restraint, are arguing that life outside the walls "with love" will surely please God much more than life within the walls without it![3]

One reason we made the movie *Fireproof* is because of our great concern for marriages. Marriage today has been cheapened. People believe if they don't get the right partner the first time, maybe they'll get the right one next time. We must pray that our kids save themselves for the right one.

8) *Pray that your home will be a spiritual haven, a fortress, and a beacon of truth and abundant life* (Ps. 19:10; 63:8; 96:3; 2 Pet. 3:18). As our girls have gotten older, Terri and I often remind them, "You can always come home." They will make mistakes, and they might make the wrong decision in some area of their lives. But we want to be like the father waiting for the prodigal. We don't want to be there waiting to give them an

"I told you so" lecture. We want to welcome our children home with the open arms of unconditional love.

This is no time for bantering about formulas or offering pious platitudes. We need more than "God Bless Our Home" on a plaque on the wall. We need something deeper than mere morality. We need moms and dads to bring their homes before God. Like Abraham, we need to put our children on the altar. God didn't want Isaac; He wanted Abraham's heart. We need homes that are one in heart and one in purpose under God. It is my prayer that every home could be a potential center for revival. If there were to be a revival in your family, it would affect your church, your kids' school, your job, and your neighborhood. If not now, when? If not here, where? If not you and I, who?

From dawn till dusk your family is being bombarded with non-Christian values. You and your spouse are under attack as well. Your children need you to intercede on their behalf. It is impossible to raise a godly generation without prayer. God may or may not bless you materially, but if God has given you children, you have something of worth on earth and in heaven. Your child is a gift from God. You have the potential to share eternity with your child. Nothing is more valuable than that!

"I have no greater joy than this: to hear that my children are walking in the truth." (3 John 4)

CHAPTER 9

PRAYING FOR OTHERS

Colossians 1, Ephesians 1

Intercession is standing in other people's shoes
and representing them before God.
—**Anonymous**

Since the day we heard this, we haven't
stopped praying for you. We are asking that
you may be filled with the knowledge of His
will in all wisdom and spiritual understanding,
so that you may walk worthy of the Lord, fully
pleasing to Him, bearing fruit in every good
work and growing in the knowledge of God.
—**Colossians 1:9–10**

PRAYER IS SUCH A VITAL PART of what we do as a church, I sometimes forget how surprised people are when we talk about our prayer ministry. Particularly surprising to people is when we talk about prayer in connection to Sherwood Pictures.

With our venture into making movies (*Flywheel*, *Facing the Giants*, *Fireproof*), we have done hundreds of interviews and been featured on dozens of secular and Christian media outlets. The stories of "the church that made the movie" have graced newspapers including the *Los Angeles Times* and *The New York Times* and television news including *FOX and Friends* and CNN.

When asked to identify the key to Sherwood Pictures and to the success we've had, the answer is simple: prayer. We pray as the story idea is formulated. We pray as the script is written. We pray during the casting. We begin every day in the shooting process with prayer and a devotional. We pray during the editing process. We pray as the movie is released in theaters nationwide. There's not a single aspect of this ministry that is not bathed in prayer.

I do my best to keep the church informed on how they can pray. One of the professionals who has worked with us said, "I've never been on a movie set where people prayed." We pray for the project, the people, and the process. And we always ask God to give us a word from His Word as we enter into each endeavor. With *Facing the Giants*, for instance, our promise was from Ephesians 3: "Now to Him who is able to do *above and beyond all that we ask or think*—according to the power that works in you" (v. 20, italics mine).

We've tried methods to change churches and people, but what most of us have not tried is prayer. I would guess the majority of churches in America have an anemic prayer ministry. They lack power because they lack prayer. They lack power because they've ignored the Word when it comes to prayer. Preaching without prayer is powerless. Prayer without a biblical foundation can become wishful thinking.

You can't separate the Word of God and prayer. Jesus said, "If you remain in Me and My words remain in you, ask whatever you want and it will be done for you" (John 15:7). Proverbs says, "Anyone who turns his ear away from hearing the law— even his prayer is detestable" (28:9).

Through the Word we are enlightened. And in praying the Word, we find enablement. The Word is our source of wisdom (1 Cor. 3:18–19). It makes our witness fruitful. Acts 2 is a testimony of the power of prayer leading to the preaching of the Word. "So those who accepted his message were baptized, and that day about 3,000 people were added to them. And they devoted themselves to the apostles' teaching, to fellowship, to the breaking of bread, and to prayers" (vv. 41–42). Someone asked the great Charles Spurgeon, "What is the secret of your ministry?" He replied, "My people pray for me."

GETTING INTO THE ACTION

One of my favorite verses in all of Scripture is found in Acts 12:5—"So Peter was kept in prison, but prayer was being made earnestly to God for him by the church." That's what we need in our churches today. Fervent prayer is the key.

Peter was in prison. He didn't need a new program, better curriculum, or a better jail; he needed a praying church. In a time of uncertainty, increased persecution, and pressure, the church turned to prayer. They were praying, knowing that at any minute Herod could kill Simon Peter. He had already killed James, so they figured Peter was next. The crisis facing the church was overwhelmingly real, yet they did not organize a protest or petition their political leaders for mercy. They didn't try to bribe the guards. They prayed. They did the one thing the enemies of God could not stop them from doing.

THEY PRAYED. THEY DID THE ONE THING THE ENEMIES OF GOD COULD NOT STOP THEM FROM DOING.

Carnal churches will acknowledge they believe in prayer in theory, but they don't in practice. The early church was a praying church. That's why sin was not tolerated (Ananias and Sapphira), evangelism was effective (three thousand saved at Pentecost), persecution couldn't stop them (they prayed for more boldness to do the very thing that got them in trouble), prejudices were destroyed (Philip and the Ethiopian eunuch, Peter and Cornelius), and missions began (Paul took the gospel to the world).

Peter would have died that night if the church had not been in prayer. The church had a compulsion and a conviction to pray. And our God is still able to work on behalf of praying people. In prayer we size up situations from God's point of view. We pray to see things from His perspective. With my sanctified imagination I can see those early believers remembering the words of Habakkuk: "I will stand at my guard post and station myself on the lookout tower. I will watch to see what He will say to me and what I should reply about my complaint" (2:1).

Prayerless churches are carnal and lack power. They are run by prayerless men and women. Jack Taylor describes prayerlessness as "that state in which one prays less than he ought, less than the Father desires, and less than that one himself knows he should."[1]

E. M. Bounds, one of the greatest voices on prayer, said:

> Prayer is the channel through which all good flows from God to man, and all good for men to men. Prayer is a privilege, a sacred, princely privilege. Prayer is a duty, an obligation most binding, and most imperative, which should hold us to it. But prayer is more than a privilege, more than a duty. It is a means, an instrument, a condition. It is the appointed condition of getting God's aid. It is the avenue through which God supplies man's wants.[2]

In this chapter I want to walk through two of the prayers of Paul and see how he prayed for the churches. Let's discover how prayer is an instrument, a condition, and at the same time the channel through which all good flows. If I don't know how to pray for someone, I pray the Word. If I don't know how to pray for my church, I pray the prayers of Paul. Why? Because I know they are inspired by God; I know I am praying with authority because I'm standing on the Word; I know that God hears because I am praying what He has revealed as His will for the church.

There is nothing outside the reach of prayer except that which is outside the will of God or the Word of God. If I am asking God to work in the lives of others, my prayers must be qualified by the following:

- Ask (1 John 3:21–22)
- Ask in the will of God (1 John 5:14–15)
- Ask in the name of Christ (John 14:13–14)
- Ask in faith (Heb. 11:6)
- Ask as a righteous man (Ps. 34:29; James 5:16)
- Ask for definite things (Luke 11:11–12)
- Ask with a grateful heart (Eph. 5:20)

I am to pray believing that God wants to hear and act.

> The eyes of the LORD are on the righteous,
> and His ears are open to their cry for help. . . .
> The righteous cry out, and the LORD hears, and
> delivers them from all their troubles.
> (Ps. 34:15, 17)

> The sacrifice of the wicked is detestable to
> the LORD, but the prayer of the upright is His
> delight. (Prov. 15:8)

> And if you believe, you will receive whatever
> you ask for in prayer. (Matt. 21:22)

God's Word clearly calls us to pray for others. The examples are numerous where we see God's leaders praying for individuals, churches, or even nations.

- Job prayed for his friends (Job 42:10).
- Moses prayed for Aaron (Deut. 9:20) as well as for Miriam (Num. 12:13).
- The prophet Samuel prayed for Israel (1 Sam. 7:5–9).
- King David prayed for Israel (2 Sam. 24:17).
- Isaiah, Daniel, and Ezekiel each prayed for God's people (Isa. 63, 64; Dan. 9; Ezek. 9).
- Our Lord prayed for the disciples (John 17).
- The church gathered to pray for Peter when he was in prison (Acts 12:5).

Knowing that God hears this kind of praying, let's turn to the prayers of Paul and glean something about how we're supposed to pray for others. You can't read Acts and the epistles without seeing the great emphasis Paul gives to prayer. Some want to get lost in the tall grass of Paul's theology, but we should also learn from him about how to pray for others.

PAUL'S EXAMPLE

Paul was a man of prayer. Ananias found him praying when he went to Paul in Damascus. He prayed before embarking on a missionary journey. He prayed in prison. Prayer was a normal part of Paul's Christian experience, his ministry, his teaching, and his daily routine. As you read the epistles, you find prayers scattered through all of Paul's writings. These prayers, remember, were a part of letters, not doctrinal studies for seminary students. These letters were written out of love and concern for churches. He would write and pray with people in mind—people he knew, people he dearly loved, people he had led to Christ.

Paul prayed for the spiritual growth of other believers. He prayed for them to have godly wisdom and understanding in Christ. He prayed that they might have the kind of unity and oneness that Jesus prayed for. If you want to invest in other believers, the greatest thing you can do for them is pray.

We can't look at all the prayers of Paul because of space, but let's look at two in particular. First, we'll examine Paul's prayer for the Colossians.

> For this reason also, since the day we heard this, we haven't stopped praying for you. We are asking that you may be filled with the knowledge of His will in all wisdom and spiritual understanding, so that you may walk worthy of the Lord, fully pleasing to Him, bearing fruit in every good work and growing in the knowledge of God. May you be strengthened with all power, according to His glorious might, for all endurance and patience, with joy. (1:9–11)

Paul continues in chapter 2 to talk about the great struggle he had for this church, striving and agonizing for them. This obviously wasn't a reference to physical work among them because he had never met them. Thus, we have to assume the agonizing and striving was in prayer. This struggle was not theoretical; it was real. Prayer is warfare.

Notice that Paul didn't just pray for a few in the Colossian congregation. He prayed that *every* member of the church would be complete in Christ. "We proclaim Him, warning and teaching everyone with all wisdom, so that we may present everyone mature in Christ. I labor for this, striving with His strength that works powerfully in me" (1:28–29).

How often we limit our praying to the willing and the remnant, but Paul never did. He prayed for the church as a whole. Oh, that we could be like Jeremiah who prayed, "If my head were water, my eyes a fountain of tears, I would weep day and night over the slain of my dear people" (9:1). The casualty count in the average church is deplorable. Why? Because we fail to bathe the church in prayer.

I have a dear friend who served as a deacon at Sherwood for a number of years. He was faithful in every service and event until a series of health issues caused him to be homebound. At one particular point of struggle in the church, he said to me, "I'm willing to die if it would bring revival to my church." God saw us through the storm. I believe this faithful man's willingness and availability were partly responsible for that.

Paul did not establish the church in Colossae, but it was on his heart. He rejoiced to hear what God was doing among them. He loved these people. His prayer for them is an example of how to pray for others—a model for praying that others might have a richer, deeper spiritual life. As far as we can tell, Paul never visited Colossae. He mentioned "hearing of their faith," and He shared with them what Epaphras had told him. But no ministry rises above the level of the praying done for it.

I know if it had not been for the intercessors in our own church, I would not have made it through some of the seasons we've faced there. That's why whenever God lays someone on my heart, I may not understand why, but it drives me to pray for them at the Spirit's prompting. I know how badly we need it, how much we depend on it, the many ways I've been kept afloat by the prayers of God's people for me.

Paul's example should challenge us not just to pray for those we know. We should pray for missionaries around the world, even if we don't know them personally. We should pray for believers in other churches, in other lands. We should intercede for those who are standing strong even in the midst of persecution.

Since 1980 martyrdom has doubled annually. There are at least 500,000 believers being killed every year solely because they confess faith in Christ. That's 1,370 a day, fifty-seven an hour, or nearly one every minute. Yet in India, they say that 15,000 a week are coming to Christ. In the former Soviet Union, thirty-five percent are now believers. In Latin America the church is growing three times faster than the population. The conversion of Muslims to Christ in the last ten years has been greater than in the last thousand years. Oh, that these reports might ignite a worldwide intercession for believers who are taking their stand for Christ seriously!

Yet sadly most prayer meetings and prayers spoken for others are only about physical needs. I call it the "organ recital." We pray for Sister Sue's toes, Brother Wally's warts, and Bubba's broken arm. While we should certainly pray for the physical needs of others, we have made prayer meetings about little else than physical needs. Surely we have time to do both—if we're serious about being involved in God's activity here, there, and everywhere.

When's the last time you were in a prayer meeting where they focused on praying for lost loved ones? When's the last time you saw a church lay out the names of backslidden members to pray for by name? In the average church we'd rather drop their names from the roll than make the effort to pray for and restore them.

The lowest attendance of any event in the average church in my denomination is prayer meeting. We moved our prayer meeting to Sunday nights before the evening service. For thirty minutes we dedicate the worship center as a quiet "House of Prayer." We give specific guidelines for prayer each evening in addition to the prayer sheet of physical needs, and we ask our members to write prayer cards. Over the years we've averaged nearly one thousand cards a week being sent out from this church to people all over the country.

Is your church open to prayer, or are you resistant to it? I can tell you it's easier for us to be like Simon, drawing a sword to cut off an ear, than it is to pray for thirty minutes. If you study the prayers of Paul, nearly every prayer is for the saints, not for the lost. He prayed for God to protect and sustain the people. Paul realized that if we can encourage more of the saints to live holy lives, those saints will be a greater witness to the lost than any tract or crusade.

PRAYING, PRAYING, ALWAYS PRAYING

We have numerous areas where we emphasize prayer as a priority at Sherwood. We have a 24/7 prayer tower where individuals and groups can gather to pray. We have a week of prayer prior to our annual ReFRESH™ Conference. Prior to my service as president of the Southern Baptist Convention Pastors' Conference, we put a forty-day prayer guide on the Web site to ask our members and believers across the land to bathe the conference in prayer.

I mentioned earlier that every Sunday morning I meet with a group of men to pray over the worship center and for our services that day. In the fall of 2008, I asked for two hundred men to join me in praying for God to move in power in our services. I found a story about Wilbur Chapman that stirred my heart to ask for this. When Chapman was a nervous young pastor in Philadelphia, he preached his first sermon. An older man came up to him and told him, "You're pretty young to be pastor of this church, but you preach the gospel, and I'm going to help you all I can." The man continued, "I'm going to pray for you that you may have the Holy Spirit's power upon you. Two others have agreed to join me in prayer for you." Chapman said, "I didn't feel so bad when I learned he was going to pray for me. The three became ten, the ten became twenty, the twenty became fifty, and the fifty soon became two hundred who met before every service to pray that the Holy Spirit might come upon me. I always went into the pulpit feeling that I would have the anointing in answer to the prayers of those who had faithfully prayed for me. It was a joy to preach." The result of those men praying was that 1,100 people came to faith in Christ in three years—six hundred of them being men. The Holy Spirit answered their prayers.

PAUL'S PRAYERS WERE NOT FOR THE SICK AND AFFLICTED; THEY WERE FOR THE SAINTS THAT THEY MIGHT BE STRONG IN THE FAITH.

In traveling around the country and preaching in conferences, conventions, and revivals, I often hear from some well-meaning soul who starts to complain about their pastor's preaching. My immediate response is, "Get people praying for him. He will be a better preacher and you will be a better listener." You love the people you pray for; you also strengthen the people you pray for.

Paul was very concerned about the Colossians' spiritual welfare and maturity. He heard of their faith, love, and fruitfulness, and he prayed for them. Again, please take note that Paul's prayers were not for the sick and afflicted; they were for the saints that they might be strong in the faith. Paul prayed for a spiritually healthy church. I'm sure there were sick people in the church, but Paul's focus was on spiritual needs. That's biblical praying because it's others-centered about things that matter for time and eternity. If God's people don't get well, they will go to heaven. But if they blow their witness, they will take others down with them.

Paul tells us specifically what he was asking God to do in them. He wanted them to have knowledge and wisdom. As you study the prayers of Paul and think about praying for others, keep knowledge high on your prayer list. Our century is filled with people who are biblically illiterate, not because they don't have Bibles, but because they don't read or think. Paul prayed for them to be completely and totally filled with a deep knowledge of God. Too many of us settle for shallow Christianity. What we need are people who will go deep with God through His Word.

For Paul, Christian knowledge was far different than the knowledge of the cults. The gnostics, for example, who often opposed Paul, used the Bible for their own purposes. The early church father Irenaeus said the gnostic interpretations were like someone taking a beautiful picture of a king and reassembling it into a picture of a fox. Paul prayed these believers would pursue and embrace the right kind of knowledge.

It's one thing to have knowledge and to know a lot of facts. I know plenty of people who know Bible facts, but they aren't spiritually minded. They know just enough Scripture to be dangerous. Wisdom is knowing what to do and how to act in light of that knowledge. Paul was concerned that the church not just be a spiritual sponge. He didn't want them to sit, soak, and sour. He wanted them to apply to their daily lives what God taught them so they would "walk in a manner worthy of the Lord."

Paul's prayer was that they know and do God's will. You can't do what you don't know. But knowing what is right to do and not doing it is a sin. So he prayed not only that they would know, but also that they would do something about it.

Take some time to look at the phrase "for this is the will of God" in Scripture. You'll discover that finding the will of God is not a game of hide-and-seek. God has revealed His will, and He wants us to know it. To know the will of God is to know the mind of Christ. If I walk in His will, my walk will be worthy of the name of Christ. This is worth praying about.

> For this is God's will, your sanctification: that you abstain from sexual immorality, so that each of you knows how to possess his own vessel in sanctification and honor, not with lustful desires, like the Gentiles who don't know God. This means one must not transgress against and defraud his brother in this matter, because the Lord is an avenger of all these offenses, as we also previously told and warned you. For God has not called us to impurity, but to sanctification. Therefore, the person who rejects this does not reject man, but God, who also gives you His Holy Spirit. (1 Thess. 4:3–8)

> Now we ask you, brothers, to give recognition to those who labor among you and lead you in the Lord and admonish you, and to esteem

them very highly in love because of their work. Be at peace among yourselves. And we exhort you, brothers: warn those who are lazy, comfort the discouraged, help the weak, be patient with everyone. See to it that no one repays evil for evil to anyone, but always pursue what is good for one another and for all. Rejoice always! Pray constantly. Give thanks in everything, for this is God's will for you in Christ Jesus. (1 Thess. 5:12–18)

Submit to every human institution because of the Lord, whether to the Emperor as the supreme authority, or to governors as those sent out by him to punish those who do evil and to praise those who do good. For it is God's will that you, by doing good, silence the ignorance of foolish people. (1 Pet. 2:13–15)

If prayer and walking with God are not important to us, they will not be important to the next generation. First John speaks to the little children, the young men, and the fathers (2:12–14). God wants us to grow up into the fullness of Christ. We aren't to live our lives as babies, content with milk. A growing Christian has wisdom and discernment. We are to pray that this knowledge and wisdom will flow and overflow. As those who have been on the journey awhile, we are required by Scripture to lead by example.

At one church I tried to get the senior adult ladies to start a program that I had heard about from Don Miller. Don called it the "Widow's Might." His plan was to get widows together to pray for one another and for the church, either over the phone or in person. It was a great idea, but I found resistance on every hand. Fewer than a dozen widows agreed to do it, and I heard some lame excuses for declining, like, "I'm not comfortable praying out loud." It goes to show you that length of years doesn't guarantee spiritual maturity.

We should be praying for others to understand the priority of their Christian walk so they can please God and bear fruit in maturity, praying that they will be able to handle the situations of life with "endurance and patience." The *Life Application Bible Commentary* notes, "Endurance is the ability to continue toward a goal regardless of the obstacles. Patience is the ability to stand firm against opposition without giving up. 'Endurance' is often used in relation to difficult circumstances; 'patience' is often used in describing one's dealings with difficult people. Both would be needed by the believers in Colossae, and both come from the empowerment of God's glorious strength."[3]

In my opinion, one of the characteristics lacking in our prayers for others is endurance and patience. We want God to answer as if we were going through a fast food line. We want people to grow up and get with it at the flip of a switch. But it doesn't happen that way. Agonizing is a part of prayer. Paul asked the Romans, "I implore you, brothers, through the Lord Jesus Christ and through the love of the Spirit, to agonize together with me in your prayers to God on my behalf" (15:30).

Notice he didn't selfishly ask for agonizing prayer for his own sake but for the sake of Christ and the love of the Spirit.

It takes more than knowledge to endure. Knowledge is not the end but rather the means to the end. Knowing God and His Word is what enables us to endure when trials come. We need to strive together in prayer if we're going to endure, grow, and mature. Knowledge exercised through wisdom enables and empowers us to walk worthy and to please God. In other passages Paul calls believers to walk worthy of the gospel, worthy of our calling, and worthy of God. Praying for others to have strength for the battle is important. We are all in a battle, a spiritual war, and the stakes are high. The saints need to be strengthened.

If the ones for whom we are praying please Him in all respects, they will live with a holy anticipation of what He wants and wills for their lives. Our desire and joy should be to please Him. Paul concludes this particular prayer talking about joy and giving thanks. Life is full of trials. We must pray that trouble doesn't make us bitter but rather makes us better.

WHERE PRAYER COMES FROM

Lastly, let's look at Paul's prayer for the Ephesians:

> This is why, since I heard about your faith in the Lord Jesus and your love for all the saints, I never stop giving thanks for you as I remember you in my prayers. I pray that the God of our Lord Jesus Christ, the glorious Father, would

give you a spirit of wisdom and revelation in the knowledge of Him. I pray that the eyes of your heart may be enlightened so you may know what is the hope of His calling, what are the glorious riches of His inheritance among the saints, and what is the immeasurable greatness of His power to us who believe, according to the working of His vast strength. (1:15–19)

Alexander MacLaren writes, "A man's prayers for others are a very fair thermometer of his own religious condition. What he asks for them will largely indicate what he thinks best for himself; and how he asks it will show the firmness of his own faith and the fervor of his own feeling."[4]

Paul began this letter to the Ephesians by instructing them in great doctrine. Now he turns to prayer, based on the foundation he had just built in the first fourteen verses. Yes, in light of these great truths, there are great prayers to be prayed. We need God to drive these truths deep into our hearts.

First, Paul wanted them to understand their blessings in Christ. They needed to rejoice in and realize their privileged position. They had been blessed with "every spiritual blessing." One thing we should pray for others is that they will understand who they are and what they have in Christ. Most of us are living like paupers when we are children of the king. Pray for believers who choose to live beneath their privileges.

Second, he prayed they might have a "spirit of wisdom and of revelation in the knowledge of Him." God's revelation of

Himself is the rock on which we stand when we pray. We pray for others based on truth, not on opinions, speculations, or preferences. Paul wanted these believers to fully understand what they had in Christ—the blessings, the power, the knowledge.

As we grow, we learn. Growth is natural for a child, so shouldn't it be natural for the child of God? If a child doesn't grow physically, we get concerned. But if a believer doesn't grow spiritually, are we equally concerned?

Secular philosophies teach us to know ourselves; Scripture teaches us to know God. This has nothing to do with IQ or educational achievements. Illumination comes from abiding and abounding in Christ. Doctrine without prayer can be dry and dull. We need both the Spirit and truth. Our prayer for others to have spiritual wisdom and revelation has one goal: that they might know Him and the hope of His calling and the riches of the glory of His inheritance. What a mouthful to pray!

We must pray for others that they might know God intimately and grow in the grace and knowledge of Jesus Christ. Paul wasn't praying for them to know more stuff but to know the Savior more intimately. J. I. Packer writes, "What matters supremely . . . is not . . . the fact that I know God, but the larger fact which underlies it—the fact that He knows me."[5] Paul's desire was to see the Ephesian believers walk in the surpassing greatness of God and His power.

Third, Paul continued by asking that these unnamed others might "know what is the hope of His calling, what are the glorious riches of His inheritance among the saints, and what is the immeasurable greatness of His power to us who believe."

What a prayer! Note that it is "His inheritance." God is the one that wills it to us. Israel was promised a land, but God Himself is our portion. We are heirs of God and joint heirs with Christ. Our inheritance is not heaven—that's a perk. Our inheritance is Christ. If heaven had streets of gold and gates of pearl but no Christ, it wouldn't be heaven. He is our inexhaustible supply.

When Paul was with the Ephesian church, he invested in them by teaching. After he left, he invested in them through prayer. Throughout his prayer Paul reminded them of the truths he had taught them. He prayed they might fully understand, embrace, and live out these truths on a daily basis. If you know who you are, you will live accordingly. You won't be tossed about by strange doctrine or feelings of insecurity. Pray for others that they will be conformed to the image of Christ and transformed in mind.

It is sad to say that most believers do not know the power available to them through the Holy Spirit. They read, "The One who is in you is greater than the one who is in the world" (1 John 4:4), but they think it applies to someone else. They walk in defeat because they don't appropriate the power that is theirs through the Holy Spirit.

Praying for others must lead us to pray that they will know the surpassing greatness of power. We often live as if God and the devil are equals, that the fight could go either way. No, Satan is a defeated foe. His destiny is set. We are to live, act, and think as overcomers. It's not that we need more power or more of the Spirit; it's that we need to appropriate what we already have available.

As you pray, do not pray for God to give others power. Instead, pray they will embrace and live out the power that is in them. Paul used the word "power" forty-two times in his letters. According to W. H. Griffith Thomas, there are no less than four comparisons stated or illustrations given in Paul's letters.

1) It is the same power that God wrought in Christ at the Resurrection. Nothing less than this is the standard of the divine working.

2) The power exercised by God in the Ascension is also intended to be bestowed on us and experienced by us.

3) It is the same power by means of which God put all things under the feet of Christ.

4) Not least of all, it was divine power that gave Christ to be "the Head over all things to the church." And it is exactly this power that is exercised on our behalf.[6]

As you pray for others, pray they will fully understand what they received when they were saved. Pray that they will have no excuses for lacking awareness of their calling, their inheritance, or their power. Pray that their Bible study leaders, pastors, and others who lead them will teach them great truths from the Scripture.

Paul wanted the Ephesians to know God's power. MacLaren says, "He was asking that their spirits should be so saturated with and immersed in that great ocean of force that pours from God as that they should never, henceforth, be able to doubt the greatness of that power which wrought in them."[7] This is our hope in a world headed in the wrong direction. We are on the right path and need to live accordingly. This is our peace in a world of chaos. This is our strength in a world filled with uncertainty. He is our strength, our refuge, and our very present help in times of trouble. Pray that others will stand and rejoice in these truths.

SO THAT THEY MAY KNOW

I'll close with a few thoughts about praying the Scriptures that I learned years ago when I first started in ministry. These have been useful to me through the years, and I believe they may be helpful to you. Start here and go further and deeper as you learn to pray God's Word.

First of all, find one of the prayers of the Bible. Come humbly before the Lord as a learner. Pray that it will be true in your own life. Read the verse and chew on it, meditate on it, let it marinate in your mind and heart. In praying these scriptural prayers, you aren't trying to get a sermon or a Bible study. Read to sense the heart of God in a word, a line, a thought, or a verse.

Then turn that passage into a prayer for others. Pray the verse back to God. Apply it to their lives. Don't rush. The Spirit may prompt you with a particular person or thought you need to camp on. Be patient and still before the Lord as you intercede. Praying the Scriptures for yourself or others is not about how much you read but about what you learn at the feet of Jesus that you can pray back to Him. Let your praying flow from the text and from the inner working of the Holy Spirit in your life.

Try this with the prayers of Paul or some familiar Psalms. Take time to read John 10 or Galatians 5 and 6 and see what God might say to you and how He might lead you to pray for others.

When we pray, our minds have a tendency to be distracted. The enemy can cause our minds to wander. We can waste time trying to figure out what to pray for. Praying the prayers of Scripture keeps us focused. Let the Scripture quiet your mind and guide it as well. Turn your heart to God and pray in full assurance of what He says. Let your mind soak in the Scriptures until out of that knowledge flows a heartfelt prayer.

Let this be our prayer that, because we commit to intercession and praying for others, it can be said of you, me, and our churches, "We always thank God for all of you, remembering you constantly in our prayers. We recall, in the presence of our God and Father, your work of faith, labor of love, and endurance of hope in our Lord Jesus Christ" (1 Thess. 1:2–3).

CHAPTER 10

PRAYING FOR THE LOST

2 Peter 3

The man who mobilizes the Christian church to pray will make the greatest contribution to world evangelism in history.
—Andrew Murray

Pray also for me, that the message may be given to me when I open my mouth to make known with boldness the mystery of the gospel. For this I am an ambassador in chains. Pray that I might be bold enough in Him to speak as I should.
—Ephesians 6:19–20

I'VE BROUGHT UP the name Don Miller on several occasions in this book because he has had a powerful influence on my life. He is a man of prayer. As founder of Bible Based Ministries in Fort Worth, Texas, he has traveled the length and breadth of this country teaching people the necessity of prayer both personally and in the local church. In the early 1990s he led a prayer conference at the church I pastor. During that conference he said, "No church can be called a praying church until it meets more to pray for others than it does to pray for itself."

One of the questions I often hear as a pastor is, "How do I pray for my lost loved ones?" I find this to be an interesting question because, by the very asking, it somehow implies God might not want to save the lost. Or it recognizes that He wants to save the lost but probably not our lost friends and family members.

There are various theological positions about salvation, but I think we would all agree that salvation is God's work from beginning to end. We are saved by grace through faith. God is the one who initiates salvation. In the mind and heart of God, there was a cross before there was ever a garden.

Is it wrong to pray for the lost? I don't think so. Look at just a few examples:

- Abraham prayed for Sodom and Gomorrah, hoping the lost would be spared if just a few righteous people could be found.
- Jesus prayed and wept over Jerusalem.

- Stephen prayed for his executioners.
- Paul prayed for Israel.

According to 2 Peter 3:9, it is not God's will that any should perish but that all should come to repentance. I'm not enough of a theologian to understand fully the doctrines of election and predestination. My purpose here is not to debate such matters but simply to encourage you to pray for your lost loved ones, friends, and neighbors. I know enough to be confident that this is in accordance with the will of God.

Paul encourages us to pray for those in authority, even though most of the people in positions of authority in our nation are likely not believers. Yet we are commanded to pray for them. I pray for entertainers and athletes to come to know Christ. I imagine in my mind the influence they could have if they came to repentance and the life-changing power of the gospel.

My friend John Bisagno shares an amazing story of the power of praying for the lost. Read his story below of God's incredible work in Ireland.

> Before entering the preaching ministry, I served the Lord for years in the field of evangelistic music. Though I was far from home without physical resources or visible hope for the future, when God called me to preach I responded immediately and was willing to trust Him in complete faith.

One evening in an upstairs room of the Belgravia Hotel in Belfast, Ireland, only two days before all physical resources would be gone, a phone call came inviting me to conduct evangelistic services. These were to begin on the following Sunday at the Immanuel Baptist Church. This was Tuesday. I accepted and began to prepare. When I called on Friday to check on the functioning of the committees and the distribution of the advertising for the meetings, I was informed that nothing had been done and that people would not be told until Sunday morning that I was to come on Sunday night.

I was disappointed, frightened, and desperately feared for the results. Realizing that only God could give a victory, I asked the pastor to call his people together at 8:00 on Saturday night for a prayer meeting. Sixty-five of us met in a small room and began to pray. One by one, hour after hour, until the early hours of the morning, they earnestly besought God for His presence and power upon the services. With my heart greatly lifted in faith, I returned to my hotel room to rest through the day.

That evening at 7:30, following a brief meeting with the pastor, we prepared to walk into the church sanctuary to begin the service.

Suddenly the pastor paused, put his arm about my shoulder, and with a look of fatherly sympathy he said, "Now, son, they don't like Yankee preachers over here. Furthermore, they have never seen an American invitation. They will not come forward as you may ask them to do. One other thing," he added, "I have not had a convert under my ministry in more than a year, and you should not expect any tonight." Then as my heart sank, he added, "And there is just one more thing, this church has never been full in the twenty-seven years I have been here, and it won't be full for you, so don't expect much."

I tried to smile and said, "Thanks." It seemed that I could never get the courage to walk through that door. I said, "Dear pastor, let us pause and pray just one more time." He prayed and then I prayed, more earnestly than I ever had, "Oh God," I said, "if I have made a mistake in following Thee, show me tonight. Let what this man says come true. But," I added, "if Thou really art God, if You still answer prayer, if I can believe and trust Thee completely in faith for everything and in every way, then I want You to show me the greatest miracle I have ever seen," and we started through the door. To my great joy I could not even reach the pulpit because of the people.

They were standing on the platform, around the choir, around the steps, in the aisles, everywhere. The church that would hardly hold 250 was jammed with 400. I preached for about ten minutes and stopped. Then I said, "If anyone here tonight is willing to receive Christ as his Lord, in faith, right this moment, I want you to come down for prayer," and immediately thirteen people stood to their feet and pushed their way forward. There was no singing, no choir, no music at all. I stopped and said, "That's all, you are dismissed."

After dealing with the seekers, I went downtown to tell the story of my conversion to about 1,200 at a city-wide, after-church youth rally. Many others made decisions for Christ that night. I went home saying, "Thank you, Lord. It was a wonderful beginning, but I still don't believe it. Now Lord," I prayed, "they don't go to church in Ireland on Monday night. I want to see it again. If you are really a God that answers prayer, do it again."

On Monday night the crowd was even larger, and fourteen came to the Lord. So mighty were the blessings of God that we extended the meetings to two, three, four, and finally five weeks. In the closing days we had to conduct two services a night to accommodate the crowds. People often stood on the steps of the church, listening through the open doors and straining to hear through the windows.

During the day we would sing and play in many of Belfast's shipbuilding yards in open-air gospel services, and oftentimes crowds of five and ten grew to five hundred and eight hundred in twenty minutes. So mighty was the power and presence of God.

One night in the services a man from Wales who could barely understand a word I said asked his sister throughout the message, "What did he say?" "What was that?" "What is he saying?" She disgustedly replied, "Oh, be quiet. He's saying something about if you want to receive Christ, come forward." Right in the middle of the service he stood and blurted out, "Oh, yes I do," and began to run down the aisle. Before another word was spoken I said, "Let us stand and sing," and with only one verse, twenty-one grown men and women in that tiny church walked the aisle after him.

People left their jobs early, merchants closed their stores, and folks literally stood on the street corners and over backyard fences talking, not about the preacher, not about the revival, but about the Lord. It is said that truck drivers and trolley operators would pass by the area of the church and begin to weep with conviction just being near the place where God was moving so mightily. After the meetings ended, I prepared to board a boat to sail to Scotland, and a curtain flung open beside the dock as over two hundred converts from that revival began to sing "God Be With You Till We Meet Again." Needless to say, that was the greatest thrill of my life. God has been with me and with them, and He is with you and will be with you in a way you have never known if you, as these people did, can learn the secret of the power of positive prayer.[1]

WHO CARES?

Clearly from John's story, God cares about the lost, and He will rain down salvation from the heavens if we seek him earnestly for the salvation of unbelievers. As a young man in the ministry, someone gave me a small tract from Back to the Bible entitled "How I Learned to Pray for the Lost." It was the first time I had ever seen anything in print regarding prayer and evangelism. Much of what I had heard regarding evangelism dealt with methods and programs. There was little in regard to prayer except the obligatory "Lord, bless us as we go out to witness in Your name."

I've got files full of programs, but they don't turn my heart toward the lost. I've been in church work long enough to know that programs and promotions won't do the job. I've seen what prayer can do. In fact, one problem we have in America is that we are so driven by the next big Bible study or conference, we run from Christian meeting to Christian conference, too self-absorbed to think about the lost.

In that tract the author said, "I have taken my place of authority in Christ and am using it against the enemy. I have not looked at myself to see if I am fit or not; I have just taken my place and have prayed that the Holy Spirit may do His convicting work. If each and every member of the body of Christ would do this, what a change would be made in this world."

Is there someone in your life who is lost? Do you love that person? Do you want God's best for them? Then plead for them. Ask the Holy Spirit to convict them of sin. Pray that situations and circumstances will be set in motion to cause them to turn to God. Take the name of that unsaved parent, child, relative, friend, or work associate to the throne of grace.

I grew up in church but didn't come to saving faith in Christ until after high school. My youth minister prayed for me because he knew I was a hypocrite. Sometimes the hardest people to pray for are those already in the church. A lot of people could be saved if they hadn't already joined the church and become convinced that church membership saves them.

SOMETIMES THE HARDEST PEOPLE TO PRAY FOR ARE THOSE ALREADY IN THE CHURCH.

Years ago a man was taken to a hospital in New York City with a slashed throat. He was a bum from the Bowery whose life was characterized by filth, cheap booze, drugs, and disease. He had been living in a twenty-five-cent-a-night flophouse, having survived on little more than alcohol for the last year. On an icy day in January, before the sun came up over the New York City skyline, the man had gotten up and staggered to the washbasin, where he fell. The basin toppled over and shattered, slitting his throat.

He was found lying in a heap, naked and bleeding from the open gash. His forehead was badly bruised. He was semi-conscious, yet begging for a drink. Those who found him dumped him in a paddy wagon and dropped him off at the nearest hospital. His name was misspelled on the hospital form and his age was incorrect. All he owned was the clothes on his back, a ragged coat, and thirty-eight cents in his pocket.

But also in his pocket were some song lyrics written on a scrap of paper: "Dear friends and gentle hearts." The injured man had written those lyrics, just as he had written other songs before—like "Camptown Races," "Oh! Susanna," "Beautiful Dreamer," and "My Old Kentucky Home." His real name was Stephen Foster, one of the greatest songwriters of his generation. But now he was dead, his body unclaimed in a morgue. Seemingly those who could hum his songs did not care whether he was in heaven or hell.

We are surrounded by people whose lives hang in the balance. They are headed toward a Christless eternity. We must ask God to give us a burden for the "least of these." We need our hearts broken over the broken lives and homes all around us. We need to get before God and pray until we see the world the way He sees it.

I'm afraid, however, that we spend much more time fretting than we spend praying by faith. The church in America is becoming ingrown because our hearts aren't burdened by a lost world. Nothing is more inconsistent with the Great Commission than an ingrown church. While the Church around the world is exploding with new converts, baptism rates among all major denominations in America are declining. We've got more money, more stuff, and more technology, but we lack the burden and thus have no power. Until we see lost people the way God sees them, we won't change. Until we change, we won't pray. Until we pray, we won't witness.

P. T. Forsyth wrote, "Prayer is a weapon, a mighty weapon in a terrible conflict. Our prayers are to be a continual, conscious, earnest effort of battle, the battle against whatever is not God's will." Again, according to the Scriptures, it is God's will for none to perish "but that all should come to repentance" (2 Pet. 3:9 NKJV). Prayer is on the leading edge of our calling in evangelism. There are more books, programs, and tracts than there are willing witnesses. While we seek new, innovative methods, God is seeking intercessors.

PRAYER MEANS YOU CARE

I was preaching in a Methodist Church Growth Conference in the Carolinas a few years ago, where the pastor told me of a bishop who serves in South America. It seems people often come to the bishop, wanting to start a church or go into the ministry. He responds to them by asking, "How many people did you lead to Christ this week?" They usually respond, "None."

He then asks, "How many did you lead to Christ last week?" The answer is the same. Then he asks, "How about in the last month?" Same answer. Then the wise bishop says, "OK, you start winning people to Jesus, then come see me in a year and we'll talk about it."

Jesus didn't see crowds of people; He saw people in a crowd. He was moved with compassion when He saw the fields white unto harvest. He then told His disciples to "pray to the Lord of the harvest to send out workers into His harvest" (Matt. 9:38). Pray for the lost. Pray for workers and witnesses. And realize that the answer to that prayer is you and me. Acts is filled with stories of evangelism, but the backdrop is a praying church.

If prayer is simply an afterthought or a supplement, it makes our methods primary and prayer secondary. But prayer is not incidental in the work of God; it *is* the work. Jesus said, "You can do nothing without Me" (John 15:5). Only in a prayer environment can our evangelistic efforts find power. One missionary said we should pray for God to give us the mind of a Baptist that we might be doctrinally straight; the heart of a Pentecostal that we might be on fire for God; and the feet of a Jehovah's Witness that we might pound the pavement.

William Law said, "There is nothing that makes us love a man so much as praying for him." Andrew Murray said, "The man who mobilizes the Christian church to pray will make the greatest contribution to world evangelism in history." We're in a battle, and we're trying to win the lost with the most undisciplined, prayerless army to ever enter the field of battle in the history of Christianity. The missionary J. O. Fraser said, "Satan's tactics seem to be as follows: He will first of all oppose our breaking through to the place of real living faith, by all means in his power. He detests the prayer of faith, for it is an authoritative notice to quit. We often have to strive and wrestle in prayer before we attain to this quiet, restful faith. And, until we break right through and join hands with God, we have not attained to real faith at all. The real battle begins when the prayer of faith has been offered."[2]

Is it really a prayer of faith if we give God an escape clause like, "If it's Your will"? Praying for the lost is something we talk about often but do very little about. Very few have boldly approached the throne of grace on behalf of the lost. We pray for the lost world in general because that's safe. We pray for missions and missionaries in general because that's safe too. But we seem to be afraid of specifically praying for specific people.

An evangelist told me about preaching a crusade in a church a few years back. As he was walking down one of the halls there, he could hear women in a side room praying and crying out to God. He asked the pastor about them. The pastor replied, "Oh, that's our women's missions group. They're praying for the heathen overseas. The problem is, I've been here eight years and not one time have they ever made it to visitation." If faith without works is dead, so is prayer without putting your feet to those prayers. Prayer and evangelism are inseparable.

Evangelism birthed in prayer is unstoppable. As you study Christian history, you see men of great prayer and faith who were used by God to shake nations. The Reformation was sparked in a prayer environment. John Knox prayed, "Give me

Scotland or I die." The Wesleys and Whitefield began historic prayer meetings that resulted in a Great Awakening. A true prayer warrior eliminates "can't" from his vocabulary.

Again, there is nothing that will make us love the lost like praying for them. We can't reach out until we reach up. When Isaiah saw the Lord, he was broken and burdened. The only way we will keep a passionate heart for evangelism is if our eyes are fixed on the Lord, high and lifted up.

ALWAYS ONE EYE ON ETERNITY

I recently pulled a little booklet off my shelf, "Reaching a Lost World," written by Warren Wiersbe when he was the general director of Back to the Bible. Dr. Wiersbe was also part of Youth for Christ when that organization first started. During those early days thousands of students came to Christ through their ministry. Warren has told me on several occasions that one of the keys to Youth for Christ was their praying. Would that describe the key to our evangelistic efforts today?

I want to quote extensively from this little booklet, long since out of print, because the message it communicates is so powerful. Dr. Wiersbe writes:

> It comes as a shock to some people to discover that Jesus Christ is not praying for lost sinners today. Many have the idea that He is interceding in heaven for the lost, but He is not. He did that on earth, where He prayed, "Father forgive them; for they know not what they do"

(Luke 23:34 KJV). But in heaven today, the Lord Jesus Christ is praying for His own.

Why is He praying for us? Because He gave us the great responsibility of reaching the lost world. Therefore, He is praying that we might get the job done. The Church is in the world, not for itself but for the sake of the lost. And our number one concern ought to be world evangelism.

For many years it has been my joy to be associated with the Slavic Gospel Association, founded by Peter Deyneka, Sr., a great prayer warrior. I can still hear Brother Deyneka saying, "Much prayer, much power! No prayer, no power!" Back in the early days of Youth for Christ, we would be in all-night prayer meetings, and Mr. Deyneka would keep reminding us, "We must pray! Prayer is what moves the hand of God!" God still reminds me, "Much prayer, much power! No prayer, no power!"

When we read the Book of Acts, we discover that the early church marched forward on its knees. They ministered with power because they prayed. In Acts 1, 120 people met for prayer, and in Acts 2, God's power came upon them and 3,000 people were saved.

When I read my Bible, I find that the great men and women of God were intercessors.

Abraham prayed for Sodom and Gomorrah. Moses interceded for Israel. Samuel said, "Far be it from me that I should sin against the LORD by failing to pray for you" (1 Sam. 12:23 NIV).

The apostle Paul had a tremendous burden for the lost. ("I have great sorrow and unceasing anguish in my heart. For I could wish that I myself were cursed and cut off from Christ for the sake of my brothers, those of my own race." Rom. 9:2–3 NIV.) Here was a man willing to go to hell so that others might be saved![3]

Dr. Wiersbe goes on to remind us that we ought to be praying not only for the lost but also for laborers in the field. We should pray for missionaries and for a new generation to surrender to missions. We should pray that God would raise up another D. L. Moody, Billy Graham, William Carey, or Bertha Smith in our generation. Maybe the ones we're praying for need a church in their area to be stirred to pray and win the unsaved. Are you praying for God to raise up people who have a heart for the lost?

Have you ever walked around a local elementary, middle, or high school campus and prayed for the students there? Have you ever parked your car in front of a preschool and prayed that those precious children would come to Christ? Have you ever asked God to show you where you can be a laborer in the fields of your community? Have you asked God to break your heart over the wickedness of sin and the callousness of your own heart toward those who don't know Christ? These are things to be praying about.

Are we crying over the things that break the heart of God? When Jesus saw the multitudes, He was moved with compassion. He wept over Jerusalem. Are we weeping over the sin-sickness of our cities? Is there ever a time when you or your church spends time praying for the city in which you live? Are we guilty of praying for God to save the heathen in a far-off land, while at the same time being indifferent to the unsaved who live in the house next door?

WHY PRAY FOR THE LOST IN THE CHURCH? BECAUSE THEY THINK THEY ARE SAVED.

How about praying for the lost *inside* the church? The church in America needs to be considered a mission field today. Far too often our members show no fruit in keeping with repentance. There is no evidence of a changed life in many of the church members in America. It's not enough to walk an aisle, fill out a form, and shake hands with the preacher. There is more to salvation than a decision motivated by regret or remorse for being caught. Repentance is a change of direction. Jesus said, "You'll recognize them by their fruit" (Matt. 7:20). If that's the case, I've met a lot of so-called Christians who only bear crab apples.

Why pray for the lost in the church? Because they think they are saved. Someone once said, "The devil spends his time telling the saved they are lost and the lost they are saved." I'm not sure how far I would take that statement, but I do know that I was once a lost church member . . . and didn't know it.

At our ReFRESH™ Conference in 2008, I saw again the reality of our need to pray for the lost. Two preachers spoke each night, with Tom Elliff and Bill Stafford both preaching on Tuesday night of the conference about being lost. Understand, now, this was a conference on revival, not an evangelistic meeting. Yet all during the service, even before invitations were given, people started coming forward, confessing their need to be saved. That night we had forty-five decisions, twenty-nine professions of faith, and twenty-one who obeyed the Lord in the area of baptism. The following night we baptized fifteen more.

Even after the service was over, people were walking back into the church to talk to someone about their need to be saved. And they didn't want to wait till Sunday to be baptized! They hadn't packed a change of clothes, but we went through every towel and robe we had. We would sing a while and baptize a while, then we'd sing some more and baptize some more. We baptized four members from one family and three from another. God just moved in and saved lost church members.

Do you have a time in your Sunday school class or small group when you pray for inactive and lost church members? If they aren't active participants, then I would pray assuming they are lost. Are you asking God to convict them of their carnality and unbelief? Are you weeping over the damage their false confession is doing to the reputation of your church?

PRAYING AND BELIEVING

Matthew's gospel tells of Jesus' compassion in seeing the crowds. "When He saw the crowds, He felt compassion for them, because they were weary and worn out, like sheep without a shepherd" (9:36). Why did Jesus feel compassion for them? Because He saw man's true condition. Beyond the façade, the stuff, the coming and going, He saw people who were frustrated, empty, hurting, disillusioned, disappointed, wandering aimlessly, and chasing after the wind of temporary pleasure.

How should we approach praying for the lost? First of all, we need to believe God.

> Is anything impossible for the LORD?
> (Gen. 18:14)

> Looking at them, Jesus said, "With men it is impossible, but not with God, because all things are possible with God." (Mark 10:27)

God's arm is not too short to rescue from the deepest pit. He came to redeem lost man. His death paid the price for sin. When we pray, we should ask for and claim all that the blood of Christ has purchased. In the King James Version, Psalm 78:41 reads, "They . . . limited the Holy One of Israel." We can limit God in our praying or in our unbelief. It's time for intercessors to believe God for the impossible and to expect the unexpected. In Matthew's gospel we read that Jesus could not do many great works because of their unbelief. Do you really believe God wants to save the lost? Do you pray believing?

Second, we need to be persistent in our praying. Salvation is not up to us; it's up to the convicting power of the Holy

Spirit. We're not trying to persuade the Lord or twist His arm. We're standing on behalf of those who are lost. It is our duty to fight for the souls of those who are lost and perishing. We wrestle not against flesh and blood. In prayer and evangelism we battle for others. So as we pray, we should pray specifically. We should pray for people to come into the lives of unbelievers who will bear witness for Christ. We should ask God how He can use us in their lives. We should pray for the Holy Spirit to convict them of sin. Let's remember that our weapons are not of the flesh. Our authority is not in our name but in the strong name of Jesus.

Jesse S. Reed said, "When we cease to bleed we cease to plead, but if we bleed and plead and do not go, we lose our concern for them."[4] Prayer is a burden until we have a burden. At the prayer conference I mentioned earlier, Don Miller gave us seven practical steps in praying for the lost:

1) Pray for them by name.
2) Ask others to pray with you.
3) Pray for their conviction.
4) Pray for a contact (this could be you).
5) Pray for them to have a seeking heart.
6) Pray in faith for their salvation.
7) Pray in thanksgiving! Praise! Claim!

I repeat again because it is so true: there is nothing that will make us love people like praying for them. Prayer is not conquering God's reluctance; it's laying hold of God's willingness.

Third, we should remember that Satan is a defeated foe. When Jesus came out of the grave, He overcame the world, the flesh, and the devil. We are called on to appropriate His victory through believing prayer. We should bind what He has bound, and we should loose what He has loosed. If it's God's will for men to be saved, then we should deal with Satan the way Jesus did. We should remember that the work of Christ is a finished work. Jesus died to pay for sin.

The lost person is bound and blinded by Satan. In one of his letters to the Corinthians, Paul wrote, "The god of this age has blinded the minds of the unbelievers so they cannot see the light of the gospel of the glory of Christ, who is the image of God" (2 Cor. 4:4). He also wrote, "But the natural man does not welcome what comes from God's Spirit, because it is foolishness to him; he is not able to know it since it is evaluated spiritually" (1 Cor. 2:14). We can pray for the lost because we know what it was like to be lost. We remember what it meant to be dead in trespasses and sin. We pray for God to open their eyes, their minds, and their hearts to the convicting power of the Holy Spirit. Jesus alone can reveal the truth to an individual who has bought into the lies of this world's system, emancipating them to a life of freedom in Christ. It's not our responsibility to "win" the lost. It's our responsibility to be prayed up and share the gospel. This is not a game we are trying to win or lose. It is a battle in which spiritual forces are raging. No one is beyond the power of God. There is no limit to what our God can do.

I encourage you to begin praying specifically for the lost during your worship services. If the altars are empty and there is no movement, it could mean that the church has not taken seriously its responsibility to share the gospel. It could also mean a spiritual battle going on for the soul of someone in your church. Either way, an empty altar should be a trumpet call to prayer. Should we not ask God to use us to share Jesus with the lost? Should we not ask God to give us churches where the sinners are loved?

You may have heard someone say, "I just don't think they are part of the elect," or "I just think they are beyond saving." I imagine someone said that about Saul before he encountered Jesus on the road to Damascus. But when Saul met Jesus and his name was changed to Paul, he became the greatest missionary and evangelist the world has ever known. We don't know who the elect are, so share with everyone at every possible opportunity in every possible way and leave the results up to God. Regardless of your theological position, your biblical responsibility to be a witness has not changed.

GETTING IT TOGETHER

In addition to its powerful prayer meetings, the Brooklyn Tabernacle is also known for the powerful conversion stories of people who have been saved out of prostitution, homosexuality, gangs, drugs, alcoholism, and every deviant crime known to man. There is power in the cross to bind Satan. Jesus Christ came to set the captives free, and we need to partner with Him in praying that the blind eyes will be opened.

In his book *Don't Just Stand There, Pray Something,* Ron Dunn wrote, "An unsaved person does not have the capacity to see himself as a lost sinner or to understand the gospel message. No amount of human power, logic, or argument can penetrate the darkness of the unsaved mind. We can't explain the way of salvation simply enough for him to believe. The devil doesn't have to make a drunkard or a murderer of a person to keep him from being saved. He only has to keep him blind to the gospel of Christ. In praying for the lost person, we are not forcing the person's will—we are *freeing* his will from the bondage of Satan."[5]

So let us pray—and then let us put feet to our prayers. It may be *us* that God wants to use in the life of that lost person. We need to always pray with the attitude, "Lord, here am I. Send me." Pray for the lost by name. Ask others to join with you in believing prayer. Pray that the lost person will come under conviction. Pray for those whom God will put in their path as a contact or a witness. Pray for more laborers in the harvest field. Pray for hardened hearts to turn to flesh. Pray in faith for their salvation. Pray thanking God for their salvation, even before they are saved.

We will impact the world with the gospel when we quit depending on programs, methods, and promotion. The salvation of the lost is not even dependent on a well-organized missions organization. The world is looking for people with integrity in their lives and love in their hearts. They will know we are Christians (and will want to know why we are different) when we love one another. My prayer is that we would find ways to cooperate with other people who are Great Commission thinkers. We don't have to agree on everything, but we can partner with anyone in reaching the lost when we all know and believe that Jesus Christ is the only way to heaven.

In the book of Acts, we see the church reaching out. In chapter 2, Peter preached to the Jews; in chapter 8, he shared with the Samaritans; and in chapter 10, he shared with the Gentiles. These accounts illustrate that the early church took seriously Jesus' words from Acts 1:8.

There is nothing more dangerous or deadly than an ingrown Christian or church. The gospel is not an endangered species to protect; rather it's a treasure to be shared. It begins in our Jerusalem. When we leave our church campuses, we are entering the mission field. The harvest is great in your neighborhood, around your church, and in your community. Don't believe for one minute that missions is something we just do overseas. Missions begins at home. The problem is not a lack of lost people; it's a lack of praying witnesses.

Could it be the difference between success and failure in evangelism is the level of praying we're doing? We've got more methods, programs, and media than ever, and yet the world is more lost than it's ever been. Paul often asked those in the church to pray for effectiveness, an open door, and protection. He even tied the provision of the Spirit and the prayers of the saints together in Philippians 1:19.

Ron Dunn clearly defined how we are to pray when it comes to praying for the lost. One, we are to pray to God—it is to Him that we pray. Two, we are to pray about men—it is for them that we pray. Three, we are to resist the enemy who is doing all he can to prevent the salvation of the lost and the spreading of the gospel. I fear that often when we are praying for the lost, we stop striving. If God doesn't answer us immediately, we quit praying. We allow the enemy to discourage us in the battle, and we believe we have no authority over him. We act as if we're praying from a defeated position.

I read an illustration of a young lady who said, "I can't get interested in missions." Another said, "No, you can hardly expect to. It is just like getting interested at a bank. You have to put in a little something first, and the more you put in—time, money, or prayer—the more the interest grows." World evangelization is an imperative because our Father said so. Prayer is an imperative because we are told to ask, seek, and knock. We are called to pray for the lost because Christ has paid for their sin with His blood. We are asking, seeking, and knocking to claim what is rightfully His.

When I was a young ministerial student at Mississippi College, I heard a man preaching on evangelism one day. He told a story I have never forgotten about Lee Harvey Oswald, the man who shot and killed President John F. Kennedy. He said when Oswald was a young boy, he walked to school every day and crossed the yard of a Baptist church on his way to school. He had no friends. He dropped out of school in the tenth grade. He went into the service and, after he got out, he became a drifter. He felt rejected and unloved. Then, of course, in November 1963, he made a name for himself by killing the president.

In 1963 the pastor of the church that Oswald had once walked by visited one of the old deacons to see if he remembered the young boy. The old deacon said, "Yes, preacher, he came occasionally, but he was a bad boy. He was bad seed. I'm glad he never joined our church."

God help us if we don't pray! If we don't pray, then we won't care. If we do pray, we will find that the God of love and salvation will give us a heart for those we would not naturally and normally love. He will put a burden in our hearts and a witness on our lips. Pray for the lost. Witness to the lost. Lift up the lost before the risen Lord, and lift up the risen Lord before the lost.

Intercession is imperative. My responsibility to pray for the lost should be unceasing. As long as there are lost people, there is a need for intercession. It is not because God has to be convinced to save the lost, but because those who are lost need the convicting power of the Holy Spirit in their lives brought on by the intercession of others. My responsibility to pray for the lost is unequivocal. It is much more than "God save the lost." It is specific, not general. It is mandatory, not optional. Praying for the lost is not the least I can do; it is the most I can do.

CHAPTER 11

BREAKTHROUGHS ARE POSSIBLE

Genesis 15, Isaiah 6, Acts 3

That which God abundantly makes the subject of his promises, God's people should abundantly make the subject of their prayers.
—Jonathan Edwards

They confronted me in the day of my distress, but the LORD was my support. He brought me out to a wide-open place; He rescued me because He delighted in me. The LORD rewarded me according to my righteousness; He repaid me according to the cleanness of my hands.
—Psalm 18:18–20

A BREAKTHROUGH is a turning point in our lives. It is a God-ordained moment when we are given an opportunity to believe God for something so great and so incredible that it can change the course of our lives, our churches, and possibly even a nation. It is when God's people are willing to take hold of the promises of God and act on His revealed will, even in the midst of unreasonable circumstances.

Phillip Brooks said, "We are haunted by an ideal life, a better world for all, and it is because we have within us the beginning and the possibility of it." To experience a breakthrough, you must surrender yourself completely. It can no longer be about self; it has to be about Him. It is getting to the point of praying, "Not my will, but Yours be done."

Breakthroughs are a big part of the stories we tell through Sherwood Pictures. In all three of our movies to date, the characters have experienced breakthroughs, pivotal moments where the story turns, the person changes, and God begins to work in and through them.

In *Flywheel*, Jay Austin finally quits playing games and surrenders his life to God at a point of desperation. While yielding his used car business to God's purposes, he prays, "Lord, it's your lot," and relinquishes his control. In *Facing the Giants*, Coach Grant Taylor turns around a losing season and comes to the realization that regardless of the outcome, he and his wife and his team will praise the Lord. In *Fireproof*, Caleb Holt experiences a breakthrough when he realizes his need for Christ and finally admits that he can't love his wife because he can't give her what he doesn't have himself.

As you read the Scriptures, you find pivotal moments in the lives of the saints. Breakthrough moments almost always come in a time of crisis when obstacles are seen as opportunities to believe God. It is a time when our faith is stretched and our hearts are challenged to ask God for the impossible.

One essential element in these crisis moments is breakthrough praying, believing God in impossible situations. In Genesis 15, we see a breakthrough in the life of Abram as God revealed to him all that was in store.

> After these events, the word of the LORD came to Abram in a vision: "Do not be afraid, Abram. I am your shield; your reward will be very great." But Abram said, "Lord GOD, what can You give me, since I am childless and the heir of my house is Eliezer of Damascus?" Abram continued, "Look, You have given me no offspring, so a slave born in my house will be my heir."
>
> Now the word of the LORD came to him: "This one will not be your heir; instead, one who comes from your own body will be your heir." He took him outside and said, "Look at the sky and count the stars, if you are able to count them." Then He said to him, "Your offspring will be that numerous." Abram believed the LORD, and He credited it to him as righteousness. He also said to him, "I am the LORD

who brought you from Ur of the Chaldeans to
give you this land to possess." (vv. 1–7)

Think about all God said to Abram that day:

- If getting out of the box is frightening to you . . . "Do not
  be afraid, Abram."
- If you're in a battle and are unsure of the outcome . . .
  "I am your shield."
- If your heart is being stirred to believe God for something
  greater . . . "Your reward will be very great."

Abram was given a God-sized vision and promise. The
breakthrough came in verses 5 and 6 when God presented
Abram with a challenge and a promise, and Abram "believed
the LORD."

Another essential when praying for a breakthrough is to see
God in your time of despair, calamity, and trouble. Too many
of God's people give up on God when they are in trouble. Ron
Dunn always said, "Anything that causes you to pray is a blessing." Have you seen your trials as opportunities for God to give
you a triumphant victory?

David did. The breakthroughs in his life are recorded in
the Psalms. Over and over we see God meeting him in difficult
and impossible situations. Psalms is not a book of honey without bees, or roses without thorns. David repeatedly saw God
break through, even in the middle of his prayer. He said of his
enemies, "They confronted me in the day of *my distress*, but the

LORD was my support. He brought me out to a *wide-open place*; He rescued me because He delighted in me. The LORD rewarded me according to my righteousness; He repaid me according to the cleanness of my hands" (Ps. 18:18–20, italics mine).

Notice the two phrases "my distress" and "a wide-open place." The word "distress" means to be in a tight place or hemmed in a corner. When the testing was over, however, David found himself in "a wide-open place." The end result of the breakthrough was that David had greater opportunities to trust God. The Lord enlarged David's trials (see Ps. 25:17) and used them to enlarge David!

HAVE YOU SEEN YOUR TRIALS AS OPPORTUNITIES FOR GOD TO GIVE YOU A TRIUMPHANT VICTORY?

The late C. S. Lewis wrote, "Hardship often prepares an ordinary person for an extraordinary destiny." It is often in the lowest times of despair and hopelessness that God breaks through and shows us a greater dimension of Himself. We also learn to ask God for greater things and believe Him for things we were once not desperate enough to plead for.

We've seen examples in the lives of Abram and David. What about Isaiah? Here we find one of the great prophets of the Old Testament crying out to God. And God shows up.

> In the year that King Uzziah died, I saw the Lord seated on a high and lofty throne, and His robe filled the temple. Seraphim were standing above Him; each one had six wings: with two

he covered his face, with two he covered his
feet, and with two he flew. And one called to
another: "Holy, holy, holy is the LORD of Hosts;
His glory fills the whole earth."

The foundations of the doorways shook at
the sound of their voices, and the temple was
filled with smoke. Then I said: "Woe is me, for
I am ruined, because I am a man of unclean lips
and live among a people of unclean lips, and
because my eyes have seen the King, the LORD
of Hosts."

Then one of the seraphim flew to me, and
in his hand was a glowing coal that he had
taken from the altar with tongs. He touched
my mouth with it and said: "Now that this
has touched your lips, your wickedness is
removed, and your sin is atoned for."

Then I heard the voice of the Lord saying: "Who should I send? Who will go for Us?"
I said: "Here I am. Send me." (Isa. 6:1–8)

An earthly king had died, and the King of glory revealed
Himself. As Isaiah saw the holiness of the Lord, he also saw the
uncleanness of himself. In commenting on this passage, Warren
Wiersbe writes:

When I was the radio speaker on *Songs in the
Night* from the Moody Church in Chicago,

I often received clippings from listeners, little items they thought might be useful on the weekly broadcast. Most of them I have forgotten, but a few of them still stick in my mind. One of the best was, "When the outlook is bleak, try the uplook!"

For young Isaiah, the outlook was bleak. His beloved king had died, his nation was in peril, and he could do very little about it. The outlook may have been bleak, but the uplook was glorious! God was still on the throne and reigning as the Sovereign of the universe! From heaven's point of view, "the whole earth" was "full of His glory" (Isa. 6:3 NIV; see Num. 14:21–22; Ps. 72:18–19). When your world tumbles in, it is good to look at things from heaven's point of view.[1]

What a breakthrough for Isaiah! With the ministry he had been given, I am sure he often went back to that moment as a reminder of God's call. It was a landmark moment that defined the rest of his life and ministry. In a year when Isaiah was broken, grieving, and searching, suddenly the Lord showed up.

ALL OF A SUDDEN

In times of desperation we need to pray for God to break through. The nation of Israel prayed hundreds of years for God's deliverance. It finally came in God's perfect timing, and they were delivered from the most powerful nation in the world. When the Israelites needed a miracle at the Red Sea, God showed up and parted the waters. When they were hungry in the wilderness, God provided manna from heaven. God sometimes seems slow, but He's never late. He's waiting on us to see our obstacles as opportunities to believe Him.

Breakthroughs can be immediate or part of a process. Sometimes when God moves, He comes in calmly like the tide. Other times He explodes on the scene like a storm surge. His moving in response to our prayers is not predictable or hurried, though it is often sudden.

The people of God prayed for centuries in hopes of seeing the coming Messiah appear. They waited, prayed, and believed that Messiah would come. Then suddenly their prayers were answered. As Malachi 3 says, "'See, I am going to send My messenger, and he will clear the way before Me. Then the Lord you seek will suddenly come to His temple, the Messenger of the covenant you desire—see, He is coming,' says the LORD of Hosts" (v. 1).

Then we read of that great moment when the angel of the Lord appeared to the lowly shepherds in Luke 2: "Then an angel of the Lord stood before them, and the glory of the Lord shone around them, and they were terrified. But the angel said to them, 'Don't be afraid, for look, I proclaim to you good news of great joy that will be for all the people: today a Savior, who is Messiah the Lord, was born for you in the city of David'" (vv. 9–11).

Note the use of the word "suddenly" in both of the passages above. The people of God prayed and waited in faith . . . and waited . . . and waited. But when God broke the silence, He did it in an instant.

Think about the early church and the many amazing accounts of God breaking through in those days. It was all the result of prayer. The new believers had been praying for days and weeks, then suddenly things changed. "When the day of Pentecost had arrived, they were all together in one place. Suddenly a sound like that of a violent rushing wind came from heaven, and it filled the whole house where they were staying" (Acts 2:1–2). The coming of the Spirit and the resulting birth of the church came suddenly. Christ had promised it. The disciples and others had prayed for it. But suddenly the Spirit broke through, and everything changed.

The conversion of Saul was sudden. Acts 9 tells us that "as he traveled and was nearing Damascus, a light from heaven suddenly flashed around him. Falling to the ground, he heard a voice saying to him, 'Saul, Saul, why are you persecuting Me?' 'Who are You, Lord?' he said. 'I am Jesus, whom you are persecuting,' He replied. 'But get up and go into the city, and you will be told what you must do'" (vv. 3–6). The greatest missionary who has ever lived was converted in an instant, in a flash of light. Suddenly the great persecutor of the church became the great missionary and evangelist.

The deliverance of Peter from prison and certain death happened suddenly. "Suddenly an angel of the Lord appeared, and a light shone in the cell. Striking Peter on the side, he woke him up and said, 'Quick, get up!' Then the chains fell off his wrists" (Acts 12:7). The church was praying for Peter's deliverance, yet they had a hard time believing it when he showed up at their prayer meeting! How often have we prayed for God to break through only to doubt His ability to do it?

In Acts 16, we read that the Philippian jailer was saved suddenly. "Suddenly there was such a violent earthquake that the foundations of the jail were shaken, and immediately all the doors were opened, and everyone's chains came loose. When the jailer woke up and saw the doors of the prison open, he drew his sword and was going to kill himself, since he thought the prisoners had escaped. But Paul called out in a loud voice, 'Don't harm yourself, because all of us are here!' Then the jailer called for lights, rushed in, and fell down trembling before Paul and Silas. Then he escorted them out and said, 'Sirs, what must I do to be saved?'" (vv. 26–30). Are we willing to go through trials, crises, and hardships if it were to result in the salvation of the lost? The early church had positioned itself to believe God to do "greater works." Oftentimes that meant a breakthrough would come as the result of persecution, but persecution led them to pray for God to do more through them.

> **GOD HAS REPEATEDLY CALLED OUT MEN AND WOMEN TO LOOK UP TO THE HEAVENS AND SEE WHAT HE WANTS TO DO.**

If you read the Scriptures and the stories of great movements of God, they often happen when least expected. We must pray with anticipation, but sometimes God surprises us. I have a friend who often prays, "Lord, today would be a great day for You to surprise me."

THINGS ONLY GOD CAN DO

It saddens me that we have limited the thought of break-throughs to the worlds of science and technology. We hear about medical and scientific breakthroughs, amazed at what is happening, yet the story of the church is nothing less than a story of radical breakthroughs. God has repeatedly called out men and women to look up to the heavens and see what He wants to do.

- Martin Luther reformed the way we thought about salvation, grace, and the church.
- Jonathan Edwards preached a sermon that started the Great Awakening.
- William Wilberforce led the way in abolishing slavery.
- George Mueller changed the way we think about faith and believing God in prayer.
- Billy Graham used television to preach the gospel, going to places no other evangelist would or could go.

These men wrestled with God and sought Him in faithful prayer. Vance Havner said, "Stay at the altar until God breaks through."[2] It is essential to His design that we come to the crisis of faith, the moment when we must get out of our comfort zone and believe Him for that which seems beyond belief.

There will be no breakthrough that is eternal in nature if we depend on worldly methods and means. What we need is power from on high. This kind of power is prayed down, not worked up. The Spirit of God can do more to change things in five minutes than we can do in our flesh in five years—in five lifetimes! Our lives, our ministries, and our churches are to be exclamations rather than explanations.

When our church began to pray about making movies, no one had heard of such a thing. It seemed insane for a church located in a predominately rural part of Southwest Georgia to make a movie, but it seemed the Lord was moving us in that direction. All the pieces were in place. We had the vision to do it, and our people were willing to serve. However, we lacked confirmation from the Lord on the project.

We never voted to make movies. I simply announced one day that it seemed God was leading us to try this. We asked the church to pray. We didn't raise a budget or take an offering, but the necessary monies came in. The result has been a breakthrough that has left many scratching their heads. How in the world can a church make a movie that gets national distribution? How can a church make movies that are now on DVD in fifty-seven countries and thirteen languages on every continent? Because a church united in spirit and in prayer asked God to use us to "reach the world from Albany, Georgia."

We simply gave God our five loaves and two fish, and He turned them into something miraculous. There is no explanation apart from God. It is beyond our ability, resources, and talents. We never envisioned in our wildest dreams something like what we've seen. We know of thousands who have come to Christ and millions who have been impacted by these films. This kind of breakthrough only happens in a prayer environment.

ONLY BY PRAYER

As I look back over these past few years and all that God has done through Sherwood Pictures, I am reminded of Daniel 12:3—"Those who are wise will shine like the bright expanse of the heavens, and those who lead many to righteousness, like the stars forever and ever." Anything not birthed in prayer and empowered by the Spirit will ultimately fail or fade.

When I wrote the book *Prepare for Rain*, several publishers turned it down because they just wanted a feel-good book about a church that made a movie. I had to remind them of the story behind the story. It took us a decade to get into a position spiritually where we could even be trusted with an idea like that. We had to go through a purging, some trials, and adversities before we were the kind of church that God would and could use to do this out-of-the-box project.

No breakthroughs come to those who spend their lives playing in the shallow end of the pool. The adventure is in the deep water where the big fish are. That's where you get a bigger picture of what you need to pray about. Your faith is never tested on the shore.

There were times in my early years at Sherwood when it would have been easier to give up, send out my résumé, and move on. If I had, I would have missed the blessing. I would have quit too soon and caved into my critics instead of staying at the altar until God broke through all the barriers that were hindering us as a church. If it had not been for praying people in the church, I might have quit. I made a spiritual application of Winston Churchill's famous statement, "Never give in, never,

never, never—in nothing, great or small—never give in except to convictions of honor and good sense."

We can't expect to ever see a breakthrough without prayer. We are to ask, seek, and knock until the answer comes. We aren't called to copy some other Christian or some other church; we are called to seek God for what He has uniquely called us to do. Instead of trying to figure out why God does great things for some and not for others, why not get before God and position yourself so He can do great things through you?

The time is now for us to get to the point where we dare not go forward unless we sense God's presence and prompting. We must pour our hearts out on the altar and set our hearts to seeking Him. We must be students of the Scripture to know how to pray biblically, not using God as an ecclesiastical Santa Claus or thinking of Him as a bellhop who jumps when we ring. The way to victory is through confession of need, through a broken and contrite spirit, and through tears. When God sees that, He meets us at the altar. He expands our borders and opens doors that were previously impossible to open.

BY HIS POWER, IN HIS NAME

If we don't seek the Lord for a breakthrough, we limit what God chooses to accomplish in our midst.

- We limit what God does in us and through us.
- We limit what God does through our church.
- We limit what happens in the future because we settle for second best.

- We limit our influence on the next generation.
- We limit our impact on the community.

I find two times in the New Testament when Jesus marveled: first at the unbelief of His own people in Mark 6, and then at the faith of the Roman centurion in Matthew 8. When I look at the anemic condition of the church in America, I think the Lord must marvel at our unbelief. We don't believe God for anything we can't ultimately do ourselves. The power of God and the refreshing winds of the Spirit do not blow on the disinterested and halfhearted, those content with the status quo.

Jesus promised He would not leave us as helpless orphans. But when it comes to prayer, most of us act like orphans rather than children of the King. We approach God apologetically instead of boldly. Some of us have even bought the lie that we would have more faith, be better Christians, and pray with greater boldness if Jesus were here with us. He *is* with us! But it isn't the physical presence of Jesus that we need. We need an awareness of His power. When Jesus ascended into heaven, the disciples started praying. And out of that prayer meeting came the promised Holy Spirit.

Jesus wasn't lying when He said, "Whatever you ask in My name" (John 14:13). He wasn't just speaking to a certain denominational or theological position. He was speaking to His followers and to us. It was a call to prioritize prayer. Alan Redpath said, "Never undertake more Christian work than can be covered by believing prayer. To fail here is to act not in faith but in presumption."

In John 14–17 Jesus mentioned petitioning the Father six different times. You don't need to be a Greek scholar to figure this out. It's simple enough for a common fisherman to understand, but it requires more faith and praying than most of us are willing to do.

- 14:13—"Whatever you ask in My name . . ."
- 14:14—"If you ask Me anything in My name . . ."
- 15:16—"Whatever you ask the Father in My name . . ."
- 16:23—"Anything you ask the Father in My name . . ."
- 16:24—"You have asked for nothing in My name . . ."
- 16:26—"In that day you will ask in My name . . ."

James warns us, "You do not have because you do not ask. You ask and don't receive because you ask wrongly, so that you may spend it on your desires for pleasure" (4:2–3). If we were honest with God, we would admit that most of our praying is selfish. "Give me . . ." "Let me . . ." "I want . . ." "I need . . ." To pray in the name of Jesus takes the focus off ourselves and puts it on His glory and the honor of His name. We are praying in the name of Jesus when we pray in agreement with what Jesus wants done on earth as it is in heaven.

Ron Dunn illustrated this so well in a story he once told about being the pastor of a growing church. Things were happening and life was busy. At the end of one particularly hectic work day, he sat down to pray. Ron realized he hadn't taken any time that day to pray or study God's Word. He had been busy, but none of it was spiritual in nature.

As he approached God with feelings of unworthiness, the first words out of his mouth were, "Lord, I know I have no right to ask You for anything tonight." He began to apologize for being too busy to pray, read the Bible, or witness.

Suddenly it seemed to Ron as if the Lord said, "Suppose you had done a lot of 'spiritual' things today. Suppose you had prayed on your knees for four hours, read the Bible for four hours, and led ten people to Christ. Would you feel more confident praying than you do now?" Silently Ron responded in his spirit, "Yes, I would."

The Lord replied, "Then you are praying in your own name! You think I hear you because of your holiness. You think I am more inclined to listen to you if you have done a lot of good works. You are approaching me in your own unworthy name. If you had prayed for eight hours, read the Bible for eight hours and led fifty people to Christ, you would have no more right to pray than you do now."

If you want your prayers to lead to a breakthrough, you have to learn to pray according to the Word and will of God, in the name of Jesus. Breakthroughs are not manipulations of the Almighty; they are a means of aligning ourselves with the will of the Almighty. Breakthrough praying has one goal in mind: the glory of God.

ALL IN

I am quite sure Peter and John had a breakthrough that day on the way to the temple to pray. Recall the events that followed:

Now Peter and John were going up together to the temple complex at the hour of prayer at three in the afternoon. And a man who was lame from his mother's womb was carried there and placed every day at the temple gate called Beautiful, so he could beg from those entering the temple complex.

When he saw Peter and John about to enter the temple complex, he asked for help. Peter, along with John, looked at him intently and said, "Look at us." So he turned to them, expecting to get something from them. But Peter said, "I have neither silver nor gold, but what I have, I give to you: In the name of Jesus Christ the Nazarene, get up and walk!" Then, taking him by the right hand he raised him up, and at once his feet and ankles became strong. So he jumped up, stood, and started to walk, and he entered the temple complex with them—walking, leaping, and praising God. (Acts 3:1–8)

I notice three things about this event. First, Peter and John noticed the man. Most likely he had been there for years. He had been there during their other visits to the temple. But on this day, they "noticed" him. Their spiritual eyes saw him. Next, they spoke to him. They grabbed his attention by saying, "Look at us." Finally, they reached out and took him by the hand. "In the name of Jesus, rise and walk." Too often we see a need, but we do nothing about it. Peter and John acted on the need they could see.

In his book *The Theory of 21*, Chuck Reaves writes, "For every one person who will say yes, there will be 20 who will say no. For a positive response, you must find the 21st person."[3] I believe part of our problem when it comes to breakthrough praying is that we are more inclined to be in the group of twenty than to be the one. If we want to see God do a mighty work, we must be willing to stand alone if necessary. Every great work of God has been done by those who believed God when others said it couldn't be done.

> **EVERY GREAT WORK OF GOD HAS BEEN DONE BY THOSE WHO BELIEVED GOD WHEN OTHERS SAID IT COULDN'T BE DONE.**

William W. Borden (1887–1913) was a remarkable person. He grew up in a wealthy Chicago family, heir to the Borden fortune. He was educated at Yale and then at Princeton Theological Seminary. As a young man he was influenced to consider giving his life to do mission work among the Muslims in China. He was ordained in 1912 and traveled to Egypt to study Aramaic in 1913. Shortly thereafter he was diagnosed with cerebral meningitis and died. In his will he gave $500,000 to schools, churches, and museums.

A note from his journal summarizes his passion. It was this attitude that helped him do what most wealthy young men would ordinarily not do, giving himself to Christ and ministry. He wrote:

Say "No" to self and "Yes" to Jesus every time.
A steep road—hard work? But every man on
this road has One who walks with him in lock-
step. His presence overtops everything that has
been cut out. . . . In every man's heart there is
a throne and a cross. If Christ is on the throne,
self is on the cross; and if self, even a little bit,
is on the throne, Jesus is on the cross in that
man's heart. . . . If Jesus is on the throne, you
will go where He wants you to go. Jesus on the
throne glorifies any work or sport. . . .

If you are thirsty, and He is enthroned, *drink*.
Drinking, the simplest act there is, means tak-
ing. "He that believeth on Me, out of him shall
flow rivers of living water. This spake He of the
Spirit." To "believe" is to *know*, because of His
Word. How shall I know that I have power to
meet temptation, to witness for Him? Believe
His Word; it will come.

Lord Jesus, I take hands off, as far as my
life is concerned. I put Thee on the throne of
my heart. Change, cleanse, use me as Thou
shalt choose. I take the full power of Thy Holy
Spirit, I thank Thee. May I never know a tithe
of the result until Morning.[4]

Borden had no idea how that prayer would be answered,
but it was a breakthrough. It led him down a different road than

others might have seen for him. To me, this prayer would make him a logical candidate for the "Breakthrough Hall of Fame" in the twentieth century. No man can pray like that without being used mightily by God.

You can stand at a river and see the opportunity or the obstacle. You can see the river and think, "It's too deep, too wide. I can't do it." Or you can say, "Lord, I believe there is something You have for me on the other side of that river. Either make a way or give me the resources to build a bridge. I don't want to die on the wrong side of the river. I don't want to live my life making excuses for why I didn't believe you for greater works." Ask God to make you willing to accomplish the difficult in order to achieve the impossible.

I would encourage you to do a personal study of the "But God . . ." moments in the Bible. These events are recorded for our encouragement, reminding us of times when God suddenly burst on the scene and redefined history.

- The ark, the flood, and the rainbow
- The parting of the Red Sea and the giving of the law
- The walls of Jericho falling down
- The defeat of the enemy by Gideon and his small army
- The cloud the size of a man's hand
- The feeding of the five thousand
- The healing of the ten lepers

Do you remember prior to the feeding of the five thousand when the disciples said of the hungry crowd, "Send them away"?

That's the easy path. That's what most of us would like to do. It's what most churches choose to do. But Jesus responded to the disciples, "'They don't need to go away. You give them something to eat.' 'But we only have five loaves and two fish here,' they said to Him. 'Bring them here to Me'" (Matt. 14:16–18).

Note the pronouns in these verses. Jesus invited His disciples to enter into a partnership with Him that would allow them to experience something they would not be able to experience otherwise. Matthew continues his account of this miracle by telling us that everyone ate and was satisfied. The disciples picked up twelve full baskets of leftovers, one for each of them who didn't believe in God's ability to do the miraculous.

If we are willing to pray in faith for breakthroughs, we have the privilege of watching God do some amazing works. But if we refuse to pray in crisis moments, we are relegated to being unbelieving, distant observers rather than believing participants amid the excitement. Pray for breakthrough!

CHAPTER 12

HOW TO PRAY WHEN JUDGMENT IS COMING

Genesis 18

God likes to see his people shut up to this, that there is no hope but in prayer. Herein lies the church's power against the world.

—Andrew Bonar

But You, Lord, are a shield around me, my glory, and the One who lifts up my head. I cry aloud to the Lord, and He answers me from His holy mountain.

—Psalm 3:3–4

ALL MY LIFE I've heard sermons on the judgment of God. I believe that because we haven't seen it in its fullness, many believe God's judgment will never come. Yet even as I write this, the news is filled with tragedy. One event after another reminds us that we live in a fallen world, a world destined for judgment.

There is a coming end.

So how should we pray in light of this? How do we pray when we already know how things will end? How should we pray for America? Can we pray for God to "bless" America when we are the world leaders in abortion and pornography? Should God spare us? How would He judge us if He decided to do so today?

When I was a kid, my parents were worried about Russia and Communism. Nikita Khrushchev, the first secretary of the Communist Party of the Soviet Union, said that America would be destroyed from within. We are hated by much of the Eastern world because they see the decadence of our society. When people flash flesh at the drop of a hat and flaunt their wealth in the face of poverty, why should we be surprised when judgment comes?

The signs are all around us that America could be crippled in the coming years. Hundreds of millions of dollars in government bailouts will not solve our problems. Sooner or later the "American Dream" could become an American nightmare. Hurricanes, tornados, and other natural disasters lead to drained resources from government agencies. Dependence on foreign oil could choke our way of life overnight. Could God be orchestrating all these events and compounding them to show us that judgment is coming?

I don't know, but I do know such news and national events should make us pause and pray about where we are going as a country.

I hear of many people who watch CNN or FOX News all day long. Most of the time the news is depressing and discouraging. But people become so absorbed in the bad news, they never think to turn off the television and get on their knees. They can't pray for others or speak for God because they haven't been with Him themselves. They know more about what a news reporter thinks about the signs of the times than they do about what God's Word says. It's as if Jeremiah was reading our mail when God inspired him to write, "Yet My people have forgotten Me for countless days" (2:32).

Jesus said, "As the days of Noah were, so the coming of the Son of Man will be" (Matt. 24:37). What were they doing during those days? Eating, drinking, marrying. They were hanging out, shopping, playing, but not praying. So no one was prepared when the judgment came.

Nothing much has changed. As long as the lights are on, our kids are happy, our rooms are comfortable, and the parking is plentiful, most churches think little about what might be on the heart of God. It must grieve the Holy Spirit when He thinks about how little we think about Him.

I do believe that God stirs the hearts of His people and often tells them what is coming. He did so in the Old Testament through the prophets. Idolatry leads to judgment. These are things that God will still not tolerate or turn a blind eye to, just as in the days of the prophets. However, this is also a great time for God to do a great work. We should be stirred to pray, not complain, moan, whine, or despair about these situations. We can't change them or control them, but we can get before God and learn how to respond in light of these events.

THE GOSPEL TRUTH

David wrote, "The secret counsel of the LORD is for those who fear Him" (Ps. 25:14). Could God trust you with a secret? Would you feel compelled to tell everyone else the secret so they would think you were spiritual? Can I tell you a secret? It's not really a secret, but those without Christ don't have a clue that we know more than they do. We are not clueless, as some suggest. God has revealed to us the mysteries of the gospel, the end times, and the coming judgment. This awareness should drive us to pray and preach the gospel as never before.

> **WE MUST NOT THINK THAT PRAYER COMES WITHOUT PLEADING.**

Charles Spurgeon said, "There is no secret of my heart which I would not pour into his ear."[1] Knowing what this world and our lost friends will face one day, we must plead with God and learn how to pray for a world headed for judgment.

We must not think that prayer comes without pleading. When we plead, we are not trying to change the heart of God. We are appealing to Him based on what we know about His character in Scripture. Abraham prayed for Sodom and

Gomorrah. Jesus prayed for Jerusalem. Paul prayed for his lost brethren. The examples are too many to mention, but you get the point.

- *Our hearts should cry out to God for help.* "I cry aloud to the LORD, and He answers me from His holy mountain." (Ps. 3:4)

- *Our hearts should cry out to God on behalf of others.* "So Moses returned to the LORD and said, 'Oh, this people has committed a great sin; they have made for themselves a god of gold. Now if You would only forgive their sin. But if not, please erase me from the book You have written.'" (Exod. 32:31–32)

- *Our hearts should cry out to God for wisdom.* "LORD my God, You have now made Your servant king in my father David's place. Yet I am just a youth with no experience in leadership. Your servant is among Your people You have chosen, a people too numerous to be numbered or counted. So give Your servant an obedient heart to judge Your people and to discern between good and evil. For who is able to judge this great people of Yours?" (1 Kings 3:7–9) "Now if any of you lacks wisdom, he should ask God, who gives to all generously and without criticizing, and it will be given to him." (James 1:5)

- *Our hearts should cry out to God for others' salvation.* "Let us search out and examine our ways, and turn back to the LORD." (Lam. 3:40) "Then he escorted them out and said, 'Sirs, what must I do to be saved?'" (Acts 16:30)

Often we find ourselves praying for people who don't even have the sense to pray for themselves. It could be a family member who is away from God; a neighbor who has a problem with alcohol; a teenager who doesn't understand the consequences of premarital sex; a family on the verge of divorce; people who are fearful of the future; government officials who are making decisions that will ultimately undermine the moral fiber of our communities and nation.

God has entrusted us with mysteries—secrets, if you will. The truths of Scripture are foolish to the lost world, and they don't understand why we do what we do. Paul reminds us:

> For to those who are perishing the message of the cross is foolishness, but to us who are being saved it is God's power. For it is written: "I will destroy the wisdom of the wise, and I will set aside the understanding of the experts." Where is the philosopher? Where is the scholar? Where is the debater of this age? Hasn't God made the world's wisdom foolish? For since, in God's wisdom, the world did not know God through wisdom, God was pleased to save those who believe through the foolishness of the message preached . . . because God's foolishness is wiser than human wisdom, and God's weakness is stronger than human strength. (1 Cor. 1:18–21, 25)

The idea that people need the message of the cross is offensive. In today's "I'm OK, you're OK" world, people don't believe they are headed for a Christless hell if they don't repent. The message of the cross is offensive, but it is a message that must be preached. We don't *seek* to be offensive, but when we tell someone they are a sinner in need of a Savior, it offends their sense of self-righteousness.

The gospel sounds foolish. After all, if there is a God and He is love, why would He send anyone to hell? The world doesn't understand that the gospel is the power of God. In the verses we just read, Paul quoted the prophet Isaiah, making the case that man's way of thinking is wrong and will ultimately fail. It's destined to be laid aside.

William Barclay writes, "If we study the four great sermons in the Book of Acts (Acts 2:14–39; 3:12–26; 4:8–12; 10:36–43) we find that there are certain constant elements in the Christian preaching. (i) There is the claim that the great promised time of God has come. (ii) There is a summary of the life, death, and resurrection of Jesus. (iii) There is a claim that all this was the fulfillment of prophecy. (iv) There is the assertion that Jesus will come again. (v) There is an urgent invitation to men to repent and receive the promised gift of the Holy Spirit."[2]

CITIES OF REFUSE

Have you ever asked yourself what God might be thinking about America today? Some have said that Hurricane Katrina was sent to judge New Orleans, but can you give me one reason why God shouldn't send judgment upon your city? The reality is that we are a nation whose cities are filled with drugs, alcoholism, rape, incest, gangs, prostitution, gambling, and every other vice known to man.

- In the town where I live, a small city in the buckle of the Bible belt, there is a "Key Club" (and I don't mean the civic organization you joined in high school). The club members are husbands and wives who put keys in a hat. Each of the men takes out a key, which determines which woman they will sleep with that night. Sin is rampant. With Internet pornography infiltrating the culture and polluting our values, should it surprise any of us if God sends judgment?

At the same time our churches are dead and dying. There is visible evidence of a lack of power in the evangelical community. Most of the growth in our churches is transfer growth. We are making little if any progress in taking the gospel to the world. Churches are dark on Sunday nights. Altars are dry and empty. Pastors are getting sermons off the Internet instead of on their knees. There is disunity within the average church. Power groups jockey for position and run off pastors at a record rate.

I agree with Leonard Ravenhill when he wrote, "To take an overall view of the church today leaves one wondering how much longer a holy God can refrain from implementing His threat to spew this Laodicean thing out of his mouth. . . . I do not marvel so much at the patience of the Lord with the stony-hearted sinners of the day. After all, would we not be patient with a man both blind and deaf? And such are the sinners. But I do marvel at the Lord's patience with the sleepy, sluggish, selfish church! A prodigal church in a prodigal world is God's real problem."[3] If that was true then, how much more today? In light of the condition of the state and the church, give me one good reason why God shouldn't judge America? It's certainly not because He loves us more than He loves other nations.

If there is not a revival of prayer and intercession, can we expect anything but judgment? It is time for the remnant to stir and to seek the Lord fervently. It is time for the old to teach the young that God is patient, yes, but He will not forever stay His hand. It is time for the church to pray for our country. Prayer meetings must turn from just praying for the physically sick to praying for the spiritually sick. When was the last time you heard someone crying out to God on behalf of the wicked in your city? It's easier to point fingers and talk back to the television than to get on our knees before God.

SWEPT UP OR SWEPT OUT?

I believe that what is on God's heart today is the same thing that was on His heart in Genesis 18. And if it's on His heart, it needs to be on our heart. We are living in an intercession crisis. There is a severe shortage of intercessors in our churches and across our land. We have tried to bring about change through the Moral Majority and similar groups formed around conservative Christian activism, yet America is worse today than it was thirty years ago. We've tried to bring about change by influencing politicians through talk radio, yet we are no better now than when we started. We've sought to elect people with our values, but they haven't been able to resurrect a decaying culture. The only thing we haven't tried, I'm afraid, is fervent prayer.

I am a child of the sixties. I was saved during the Jesus Movement. When it swept through the sleepy little town of Pascagoula, Mississippi, my youth minister James Miller started having youth prayer meetings in the church. Of course our deacons—"men full of faith, wisdom, and the Holy Spirit"—had to approve our use of the sanctuary because the additional use of electricity wasn't in the budget. If I remember correctly, we started with about six people, including the youth minister. What started as two nights a week soon grew to every night during that summer. At its peak we would have several hundred students present and praying.

There was no Bible study or praise team. We sang a little, then prayed and sat quietly until someone else started praying, until there was finally a sense that it was time to leave. Some nights I remember going home at two or three in the morning.

The great changes in American culture happened during the Awakenings of the 1700s and 1800s, and we haven't seen an awakening or a national revival in America since. I believe God's desire was to bring about a great movement of the Holy Spirit during the days of the Jesus Movement. But by and large, the church in America was resistant. Stuart Briscoe wrote a book at the time entitled *Where Was the Church When the Youth Exploded?* The status quo crowd didn't want converted hippies and drug addicts messing up their lovely facilities.

While major publications like *Time, Newsweek, Life,* and *Look* all featured stories on the movement, the church was silent, indifferent, and unwilling to change. Some have blamed the hippies for the state of America today. I blame the church.

At a time when God was moving among students to counter the "tune in, turn on, drop out" mind-set of the late 1960s, the church typically resisted the work of God. I had one lady in my church tell me, "You'll get over it." I never have. What I did get over was lifeless, boring religion that is prayerless and powerless.

During those days I saw guys and gals walk into the prayer meeting (some not even knowing why they were there) and fall under conviction. I saw people delivered from drugs on the spot because of the presence of God and the prayers of a bunch of students. I watched people weep their way into the presence of God. We were just silly enough to believe that He heard us when we prayed, along with a small number of spiritual adults who encouraged us to step out and believe God for "greater works."

It does grieve me to think that, for the most part, my home church was clueless as to what was happening. They didn't even bother to check it out. Few ever encouraged us. If it hadn't been for a few youth workers who stood with us and believed in us, the movement would have died before it even got started. I'll be eternally grateful for James and that handful of adults who believed God was moving and who spurred us to get in on what God might be doing. I live and long for another wind of the Spirit like I experienced in those days. If the church in America does not pray for a revival, we will preside over a funeral.

In his excellent book *The Choice: America at the Crossroads of Ruin and Revival*, Sammy Tippet wrote:

I have had to ask myself, "Why didn't the Jesus Movement become that which turned the moral and spiritual tides in those critical days of American history?" If there is to be a national revival, then we must return to the root cause of our falling away. America turned away from the Bible as its basic foundation in the '60s, and only a movement centered in strong Biblical teaching and discipleship would be able to turn the tide of relativism in the nation.

Second, there wasn't a strong call for repentance in many circles. There was too much "get high on Jesus" theology and not enough preaching the message of Christ. . . . Finally, churches weren't prepared for the harvest. In the words of Jesus, we need a "wineskin" able to hold "the new wine."[4]

BEGGING AND PLEADING

In Genesis 18 we find the first recorded prayer in the Bible. It is an intercessory prayer in the context of God's coming judgment on Sodom and Gomorrah. Nothing is so offensive to godless people as the message of intercession. I would submit that the people in the region of Sodom were without excuse. They had seen the goodness of God, and yet they refused to change their ways.

When they were defeated by the four kings of the East, God delivered them through Abraham. They were grateful, but they didn't change. They had heard the testimony of Melchizedek, but they didn't change. Surely at first, Lot had given the area some kind of witness, but soon he caved in to the culture and mixed in with the crowd.

> Then the LORD said, "Should I hide from Abraham what I am about to do?". . . Then the LORD said, "The outcry against Sodom and Gomorrah is immense and their sin is extremely serious. I will go down to see if what they have done justifies the cry that has come up to Me. If not, I will find out."
>
> The men turned from there and went toward Sodom while Abraham remained standing before the LORD. Abraham stepped forward and said, "Will You really sweep away the righteous with the wicked? What if there are 50 righteous people in the city? Will You really sweep it away instead of sparing the place for the sake of the 50 righteous people who are in it? You could not possibly do such a thing: to kill the righteous with the wicked, treating the righteous and the wicked alike. You could not possibly do that! Won't the Judge of all the earth do what is just?" (vv. 17, 20–25)

God told Abraham a secret. He revealed to Abraham what He was about to do. We can obviously assume that Abraham was aware of the ungodliness of the cities, but at this point God took that awareness and turned it into a call to prayer. Every time you see fellowship between God and Abraham, God is the one who starts the conversation.

Prayer is not so much talking to God as it is God speaking to us and telling us what is on His heart. I remember hearing E. V. Hill, a great African-American preacher from Los Angeles, speak at the Billy Graham School of Evangelism in Jackson, Mississippi, in 1975. He said, "If you get people talking to God, God will tell them what is on His heart. And what is on His heart is a lost world." Could it be that our lack of compassion and concern for the lost is the result of our lack of genuine praying? God is trying to speak, but are we listening? It's God's prerogative to speak, but it's our responsibility to listen and respond accordingly.

Abraham had no idea how many righteous people there might be in Sodom. He obviously knew he had family there. The prayer in Genesis 18 is from a man who cares deeply about others—some he knew and some he didn't know. But the revelation caused him to turn to intercession.

Herbert Lockyer reminds us:

> Facing the desolating fury of a justly indignant God, Abraham had one resort, one privilege— he could *pray* for guilty Sodom. With his prayer commences one of the most remarkable instances of human intercession to be met with in the whole compass of divine revelation. . . .

Abraham for Sodom proves: 1) The benevolence of good men. 2) The importance of the righteous in a wicked world. 3) The kindness of God towards the guilty. 4) The humility which should ever characterize prayer. 5) The efficacy of intercessory prayer. Such prayer is ever costly—it is the saint's sweat of soul. Abraham carried on his heart the sins and sorrow of Sodom. He "sat where they sat." But there came a point when his intercession ceased. When God has finally determined the ruin of a place, He forbids it to be prayed for. [5]

Note these words from the prophet Jeremiah about when it's time to stop praying for those under judgment.

"As for you, do not pray for these people. Do not offer a cry or a prayer on their behalf, and do not beg Me, for I will not listen to you. Don't you see how they behave in the cities of Judah and in the streets of Jerusalem? The sons gather wood, the fathers light the fire, and the women knead dough to make cakes for the queen of heaven, and they pour out drink offerings to other gods so that they provoke Me to anger. But are they really provoking Me?" This is the Lord's declaration. "Isn't it they themselves being provoked to disgrace?" Therefore, this is what the Lord God says: "Look, My anger—My burning wrath—is about to be poured out on this place, on man and beast, on the tree of the field, and on the fruit of the ground. My wrath will burn and not be quenched. (7:16–20)

Then the Lord said to me, "Do not pray for the well-being of these people. If they fast, I will not hear their cry of despair. If they offer burnt offering and grain offering, I will not accept them. Rather, I will finish them off by sword, famine, and plague." (14:11–12)

A man came to my office one day to tell me his family was leaving our church. As we started the conversation, he said, "I've been committed to this church, and I'm committed to reaching people for Christ. I think no one could question my commitment to evangelism." For the life of me, I've not found one person in this church family who came to Christ through his witness. Although I can recall countless times when our church prayed for him and *his* family, I can't recall one time when he was involved in our intercessory prayer ministry.

If we have the heart of God, we will be burdened for the things He is burdened about. He is burdened for souls. And until He tells you to stop praying for your lost friends, relatives, neighbors, and community, keep praying. Don't shrug your shoulders at a coming judgment and try to justify disobedience to clear examples of Scripture.

TAKING A KNEE, TAKING A STAND

God was on the verge of destroying Sodom and Gomorrah in a single stroke of judgment. From the biblical account it seems He was having a conversation in heaven and decided to let Abraham in on what He was about to do. God had a purpose in judging and in revealing the coming judgment to Abraham. God doesn't have favorites, but He does have intimates. He could have told Lot, but he wasn't spiritually ready to listen. So God told Abraham. Why? "For I have chosen him . . ."

This raises the level of prayer from petty needs to praying through God's agenda. This revelation resulted in Abraham's standing on the mountain and interceding for the people in the plains. They might not have been willing to listen to a sermon, but they couldn't stop a prayer. Charles Spurgeon said: "If they [lost sinners] will not hear you speak, they cannot prevent your praying. Do they jest at your exhortations? They cannot disturb you at your prayers. Are they far away so that you cannot reach them? Your prayers can reach them. Have they declared that they will never listen to you again, nor see your face? Never mind, God has a voice which they must hear. Speak to Him, and He will make them feel. Though they now treat you despitefully, rendering evil for your good, follow them with your prayers. Never let them perish for lack of your supplications.[6]

GOD DOESN'T HAVE FAVORITES, BUT HE DOES HAVE INTIMATES.

Abraham had reasons to take up this burden. First of all, his nephew Lot lived in the city. What affected that city would affect his family. Second, he believed there might be other righteous people in the city. He thought there would be at least fifty. Third, he had compassion. Even though it was obvious these people in their hedonism and godlessness deserved judgment, Abraham called on God to be gracious.

When you pray for a city or for people who are racing toward judgment, you must have the right heart and motive. We know that God "wants everyone to be saved and to come to the knowledge of the truth" (1 Tim. 2:4). We understand that He is "not wanting any to perish, but all to come to repentance" (2 Pet. 3:9). Sodom may mean nothing to us, but to Abraham it was a city filled with people, many of whom he would have known. For believers it is imperative that we ask God to give us broken hearts for those who are lost, deceived by the Deceiver, and blinded by the one who appears as an Angel of Light.

You could say the destruction of Sodom was a foreshadowing of the coming flood. God was sending a clear signal that sin would be judged. Small judgments are a reminder that there will come a day when bigger judgments are rendered.

God never specifically told Abraham He was going to destroy the city. He merely revealed to Abraham how wicked their condition was. He said their sin was "grievous." God sees and knows. There is a coming day of judgment.

WHAT ARE WE ASKING FOR?

My wife and I made a trip out west in the summer of 2008. We drove through New Mexico, Colorado, Utah, Nevada, and Arizona. We spent three days in Las Vegas. We are the kind of tourists they hate in Vegas. We stayed in a nice hotel, but we didn't smoke, gamble, or drink.

One thing I can tell you about Las Vegas: the overwhelming majority of people who visit there are empty inside. They're looking for truth in a bottle or at the bottom of a shot glass. They put their hope in luck, trying to find the answer to the emptiness of their soul in a slot machine. They may be drinking, laughing, and partying, but inside they are crying out for something to fill the void in their lives. They are looking for a stimulant. What they need is a Savior.

But I've discovered that there are also some great churches with great ministries in Sin City, actively involved in reaching that community for Christ. Several have thousands in their weekend services. We may be appalled at the godlessness of the city, but have our hearts been broken over it? Have we ever interceded for the believers who live there to be salt and light?

To be biblical intercessors we first need to make sure we are praying the will of God as best we understand it. We must filter our praying through the grid of Scripture. It's not about what we want to see happen; it's about getting so in tune with heaven that we sense the mind and heart of God. Second, we need to aggressively cooperate with God. Intercessory prayer is not passive. We need to grab hold of the throne of grace on behalf of others.

Oswald Chambers said, "We have not the remotest conception of what is done by our prayers, nor have we the right to try and examine and understand it; all we know is that Jesus Christ laid all stress on prayer."[7] Our job is to pray; God's job is to answer. Our job is to ask, seek, and knock; God's job is to open. Our job is to respond properly when God reveals Himself.

It has been said that when Abraham stood before God, he was in a position of partnership, a position of fellowship, and a position of stewardship. He was God's man for the hour. Ron Dunn said, "Intercession is more than prayer. Prayer is a form and expression of intercession, but it alone is not intercession. Intercession is not petition. Intercession is position. It is not something we do—it is something we are. It is not an exercise we engage in at a certain time of day—it is a life that we live."

Someone once said, "Our position is *before* God and *between* God and the person we are interceding for. Abraham stood *before* the Lord and *between* the Lord and Sodom." John Phillips wrote, "He took up his position, his thought full of Lot, down there in Sodom. He stood, as it were, between the living and the dead, taking up his stand on redemption ground; prepared to plead and plead for Sodom because of Lot. It was holy boldness in the highest degree. Abraham had now become more Christlike than ever; he had become a mediator between God and man."

Genesis 18:27 reveals Abraham's frame of mind as he prayed: "I have ventured to speak to the Lord—even though I am dust and ashes." Abraham was aware of the ground he was standing on. He wasn't cocky. He wasn't unaware of the realm he had entered into. He didn't strut before sovereignty. He came before God humbly and with reverence. He also stood before God fully aware of the problem. Ephesians 2 tells us that by nature men are "children under wrath" (v. 3). In Romans,

Paul reminds us that "God's wrath is revealed from heaven against all godlessness and unrighteousness of people who by their unrighteousness suppress the truth" (1:18).

Intercessory prayer is hard work.

But have we become so busy that we limit praying for our cities and our nation to the National Day of Prayer? Yes, it's great that we spend a day focusing on praying for our nation. But we are to pray every day for those in authority. We are to pray for the lost. We are to pray for the backslidden and carnal. It is a sin to say "Thy will be done" if there has been no intercession. God expects us to be prayer warriors, not judges. The reason we pray is because God has told us to—not to get the answers we want but to obey the Lord who has called us to be a praying people.

> Then Abraham answered, "Since I have ventured to speak to the Lord—even though I am dust and ashes—suppose the 50 righteous lack five. Will you destroy the whole city for lack of five?" He replied, "I will not destroy it if I find 45 there." Then he spoke to Him again, "Suppose 40 are found there?" He answered, "I will not do it on account of 40." Then he said, "Let the Lord not be angry, and I will speak further. Suppose 30 are found there?" He answered, "I will not do it if I find 30 there." Then he said, "Since I have ventured to speak to the Lord, suppose 20 are found there?" He replied, "I will

not destroy it on account of 20." Then he said,
"Let the Lord not be angry, and I will speak
one more time. Suppose 10 are found there?"
He answered, "I will not destroy it on account
of 10." When the Lord had finished speaking
with Abraham, He departed, and Abraham
returned to his place. (Gen. 18:27–33)

It was because of the words recorded in Genesis 18 that the
English evangelist and orphanage founder George Mueller was
moved to become an intercessor. He testified that it taught him
to use "argument" in pleading his case before God. He would
remind God of his need and of God's promises. Mueller said the
secret to intercession and pleading before God was to have faith
in God. Some have said that in his lifetime Mueller recorded
over 25,000 answers to prayer.

Abraham was not guilty of meaningless repetition. He
wasn't pestering God. He was persistent in seeking to grasp what
God was going to do. He had been invited by the Lord God
Almighty to pray, so he prayed. God invited Abraham to keep
asking because He kept answering "yes" every time Abraham
brought a new petition before Him. Six times he prayed for
Sodom, and six times God gave an affirmative answer on the
spot. The Lord didn't stop saying "yes" until Abraham stopped
asking. Because Abraham was so in tune with the Lord on this,
I believe he sensed in his heart there wouldn't even be ten.

I remember when I first spent time with the woman who
would one day become my wife. I had seen Terri at our youth

prayer meetings, but she went to a different school. One night we went on a double date, but we were not together. I had been dating a friend of Terri's, and she had a date with a guy I went to school with. About halfway through the evening, I was struck by her presence. There was something about her smile, her spirit, and her love for the Lord that made her stand out above every other girl I had ever dated.

It wasn't intentional, but it appeared mutual. We began talking through dinner and the drive home and, I must confess, we both ignored our dates. It didn't take me long to figure out I wanted to ask Terri out on a date myself. I would see her driving up and down the "main drag" in our small town and wonder if she would ever go out with me.

One night a friend and I walked into the local Pizza Hut, and there she was. We sat down to order, but she got up and left, so we followed her and her friend down the street to the Burger King. Over the next forty-five minutes I asked her out three times, and she turned me down each time. Finally she gave in to my persistence, and the rest is history. Nearly forty years later, we are still together.

What if I had given up on the first request? What if I had said, "She's not worth the effort"? What if I had decided her first response would be her last response? Isn't that how we pray at times? Our tendency as believers is to stop short of seeing God work. We might pray for a lost or backslidden friend for a few weeks, but if nothing changes, we stop praying. Rather than intensifying our efforts, we back off as if God is not interested or capable of changing the situation.

It's always too soon to stop believing. It's too soon to stop pleading, unless God has spoken to your heart about the matter and has given you His mind on the matter.

I have a friend who recently preached the funeral of an uncle they had prayed for more than fifty years to be saved. On the last Monday of the man's life, he had a heart attack. On that day he gave his life to Christ, then died three days later. What if the family had not been persistent in prayer? Yes, I know God is sovereign. But the question comes: Are we persistent?

Oswald Chambers wrote, "By intercessory prayer we can hold off Satan from other lives and give the Holy Spirit a chance with them."[8] We know that God judges personal, corporate, and national sin. But we also know God delays judgment and gives us an opportunity to partner with Him in believing prayer. Intercessory prayer is part of the sovereign work of God. He has chosen to limit Himself, in some ways, to prayer.

> Oh, to pray so as to be known in hell! / Oh, to pray so that demons have to quit their prey! / Oh, to cause pandemonium in perdition when we intercede! / Oh, to liberate the captives when we make intercessions with tears! / Oh, to push the devil around instead of his pushing the Church around! / Oh, to know the groanings that cannot be uttered![9]

ACKNOWLEDGMENTS

When I think of prayer, I think of the people who have undergirded my life with prayer. I think of those who worked and served in the preschool and children's ministries when I was growing up. Only eternity will reveal what their prayers did for me and what they protected me from. They are the unknown intercessors of my early years.

Then I think of the lay people I've been privileged to minister with during nearly forty years of ministry. These men and women have placed my name before the Lord in ways I will never fully know and can never repay. They have prayed for me to mature as a man of God. They have prayed for me as a husband, father, and minister. They have lifted my name to the Lord at times when I wasn't even aware of it.

In some ways, everything God has done through my ministry has been because of people moving me forward on their knees. I know there has never been a day when I have not been prayed for. When I was a lost church member as a teenager, my youth minister and twelfth grade Sunday school teacher prayed for me. My parents prayed for me. I have little spiritual heritage in my family, as most of my family were either lost or casual church members. But I know my parents prayed for God to use me when I surrendered to the ministry. I also have a wife who knows me at my best and worst and still prays for me.

The work of God cannot be done in the energy of the flesh. It must be bathed in prayer. I've had the privilege of leading two churches to start an intercessory prayer ministry. I believe the depth of our prayer ministry determines in large part the breadth and height of our influence as a church.

I've had a prayer group at Sherwood since 1992. These men meet with me every week that I am in town. They know me, warts and all. One of these men, Roy Pippin, is no longer able to attend due to health reasons, but I sense his prayers. The other two, John Dees and Ron Dorminey, have been stalwart warriors on my behalf. I would have already crashed and burned if not for their belief in me. They have been my Aaron and Hur.

I am grateful to those who are a part of the prayer ministry in its various forms at Sherwood. We have hundreds involved in our 24/7 prayer ministry. Every Sunday morning, men meet me at 7:45 to pray at the altar for me and the services that day. While I'm preaching, men and women gather in "Spurgeon's Closet" underneath the choir loft to pray for the services.

In addition, I am privileged to have nearly two hundred praying men I e-mail each week with specific requests. These men and women in the above-mentioned groups are all part of an army of prayer warriors who understand that prayer is not optional—it is essential.

In no way do I consider myself an authority on prayer. When I look on my shelves at the books on prayer written by holy, godly, praying men, I wonder what I've got to say that hasn't already been said. In reality, any book on prayer is just a reminder of old truths often forgotten. In our busyness we tend to forget the business of the church: "My house shall be called a house of prayer." In believing prayer we exercise our faith in a God who hears and answers.

I must acknowledge a few folks who have made this project what it is. First of all, the team at B&H Publishing Group has been a blessing to work with. They have prayed fo me and worked to insure that these books in the ReFRESH™ Series are as good as they can be. Their input, editing, suggestions, and creativity are greatly appreciated. It's fun to work with folks who see the need for this kind of book.

Stephanie Bennett has been my research assistant since she graduated from New Orleans Seminary. I've known her since she was in the third grade. She has skills and abilities I lack, and she makes me look like a better writer than I really am.

Debbie Toole has been my administrative assistant for nearly twenty years. She keeps my crazy travel plans and appointments organized so I have time to write. If she weren't on top of her responsibilities, I would never have time to get to my study and work on sermons and books. Her many contributions to my life and ministry are invaluable.

To those who have allowed me to use their stories in this book, I am grateful. People love a good story. But I think you'll agree that these aren't just good stories; they're the stories of great people and an even greater God.

To my wife, Terri, and my two girls, Erin and Hayley, I say thanks. You've believed in me when at times I didn't believe in myself. I pray I've not neglected you in the crunch of writing these pages. My prayer is that Erin and Hayley will continue the heritage of faith and faithfulness that Terri and I have sought to establish.

The greatest thrill for me is not that I have been able to speak in large conferences or appear on numerous secular and religious TV and radio shows because of Sherwood Pictures. The greatest thrill for me is being a part of a praying church. It's not that prayer enables us to do a greater work; prayer is the greatest work we do. S. D. Gordon said, "You can do more than pray *after* you have prayed, but you cannot do more than pray *until* you have prayed."

Most of all, I acknowledge my everlasting gratitude to the Lord Jesus who "ever lives to make intercession for me." To know that Jesus is praying for me right now is a thought beyond my comprehension. I embrace it as a treasure that I never take for granted. He's praying for me. He's praying for you. And I pray He has spoken to you as you've read these pages.

—Michael Catt
    Albany, Georgia
    May 2009

NOTES

CHAPTER 1

1. *Spurgeon's Sermons on New Testament Women* (Grand Rapids, MI: Kregel, 1994), 127.

2. *The Life Application Bible Commentary Series* (Carol Stream, IL: Livingstone Corporation, produced with permission of Tyndale House Publishers, Inc., 1997).

3. Raymond Edman, *They Found the Secret* (Grand Rapids, MI: Zondervan, 1966).

4. Ibid, 78–80.

CHAPTER 2

1. C. S. Lewis, *Reflections on the Psalms* (New York: Harcourt, Brace & World, 1958), 132.

2. Donald Grey Barnhouse, *God's Glory: Exposition of Bible Doctrines* (Grand Rapids, MI: Eerdmans, 1964), 72–73.

CHAPTER 4

1. Quoted in *Pocket Handbook of Christian Apologetics*, Peter Kreeft and Ronald Tacelli (Downers Grove, IL: InterVarsity, 2003), 29.
2. *Fullness Magazine*, January/February 1983, 16.
3. Jeffrey L. Sheler, "The Power of Prayer," *U.S. News & World Report*, December 12, 2004.
4. *Fullness Magazine*, January/February 1983, 20. Adapted from *The Prayer Life* by Andrew Murray (Chicago: Moody Press, 1985).
5. Jim Cymbala, "How to Light the Fire," *Leadership Magazine*, October 1, 1994.
6. John Calvin, *Commentary on a Harmony of the Evangelists, Matthew, Mark and Luke* (Grand Rapids: Christian Classics Ethereal Library), accessed via the Internet at www.ccel.org.
7. William Barclay, *The Gospel of Luke: The New Daily Study Bible* (Louisville: Westminster John Knox Press, 2001), 174.

CHAPTER 5

1. James Montgomery Boice, *Boice Expositional Commentary, The Gospel of Matthew, Volume 1: The King and His Kingdom (Matthew 1–17)*, accessed via WORDsearch Bible Software.
2. Lehman Strauss, *Sense and Nonsense About Prayer* (Chicago: Moody Press, 1974), 93.
3. Donald English, *Ten Praying Churches* (Derby, CT: Monarch Books, 1989), 7–8.
4. Warren Wiersbe, *The Bible Exposition Commentary: New Testament, Volume 1* (Victor Books, 2004).

5. Gene Mims, *The Kingdom Focused Church* (Nashville: Broadman & Holman, 2003), 41.

CHAPTER 6

1. Isaac David Ellis Thomas, ed., *Golden Treasury of Puritan Quotations* (Chicago: Moody Press, 1975), 103.

2. W. Robertson Nicoll, ed., *Expositor's Dictionary of Texts*, (London: Hodder & Stoughton).

3. John Bisagno, *The Secret of Positive Praying* (Grand Rapids: Zondervan, 1986), 162.

CHAPTER 7

1. *Warfighting* (U.S. Marine Corps, 1989).

2. John MacArthur, *How to Meet the Enemy* (Wheaton, IL: Victor Books, 1992), 19.

3. *Warfighting*, 7.

4. Vance Havner, *Pepper 'n' Salt* (Old Tappan, NJ: Fleming H. Revell Company, 1966), 18.

5. A. W. Tozer, *The Warfare of the Spirit* (Christian Focus Publications, 1993), 3–4.

6. H. A. Ironside, *Ephesians: An Ironside Expository Commentary* (Grand Rapids: Kregel Publications, 2007).

7. Warren Wiersbe, *The Strategy of Satan* (Carol Stream, IL: Tyndale House, 1979), 136.

8. James Philip, *Christian Warfare and Armour* (Ft. Washington, PA: Christian Lit. Crusade, 1972), 115.

9. Strauss, *Sense and Nonsense About Prayer*, 122.

CHAPTER 8

1. G. Michael Cocoris, *Evangelism: A Biblical Approach* (Chicago: Moody Press, 1984), 108.
2. Jack Taylor, *One Home Under God* (Nashville: Broadman Press, 1974), 95.
4. Jill Briscoe, *Fight for the Family*, (Grand Rapids: Zondervan, 1981), 29.

CHAPTER 9

1. Jack Taylor, *Prayer: Life's Limitless Reach* (Nashville: Broadman Press, 1977), 35.
2. Leonard Ravenhill, *A Treasury of Prayer* (Fires of Revival Publishers, 1961), 37.
3. *The Life Application Bible Commentary Series* (Carol Stream, IL: Livingstone Corporation, produced with permission of Tyndale House Publishers, Inc., 1997).
4. Alexander MacLaren, *Paul's Prayers and Other Sermons* (London: Alexander & Shepheard, 1892), 47.
5. J. I. Packer, *Knowing God* (Downers Grove, IL: InterVarsity Press, 1973), 37.
6. W. H. Griffith Thomas, *The Prayers of St. Paul* (New York: Scribner's Sons, 1914), 104–105.
7. MacLaren, 74.

CHAPTER 10

1. John R. Bisagno, *The Power of Positive Praying* (Xulon Press, 2005), used by permission.

2. http://www.epm.org/artman2/publish/prayer/Great_Quotes_
   On_Prayer.shtml

3. Warren Wiersbe, *Reaching a Lost World* (Lincoln, NE:
   Back to the Bible, 1989).

4. James Ponder, *Evangelism Men: Motivating Laymen
   to Witness* (Nashville: Broadman Press, 1974).

5. Ron Dunn, *Don't Just Stand There, Pray Something!*
   (Billy Graham Evangelistic Association, 1992).

CHAPTER 11

1. Warren Wiersbe, *The Bible Exposition Commentary:
   Old Testament* (accessed via PC Study Bible).

2. Vance Havner, *By the Still Waters* (New York:
   Fleming H. Revell, 1934), 10.

3. Chuck Reaves, *The Theory of 21* (Advantage Books, 2005).

4. Howard Taylor and Mary Geraldine Taylor, *Borden of Yale:
   A Life That Counts* (China Inland Mission, 1957), 122–123.

CHAPTER 12

1. Tom Carter, *Spurgeon at His Best* (Grand Rapids: Baker
   Books, 1988), 142.

2. William Barclay, *The Acts of the Apostles: The New Daily
   Study Bible* (Louisville: Westminster John Knox Press,
   2003), 29–30.

3. Leonard Ravenhill, *Why Revival Tarries* (Bethany
   Fellowship, 1959), 97–98.

4. Sammy Tippet, *The Choice: America at the Crossroads of
   Ruin and Revival* (Chicago: Moody Press, 1998), 159–160.

5. Herbert Lockyer, *All the Prayers of the Bible* (Grand Rapids: Zondervan, 1959), 23–24, 160.

6. Charles Spurgeon, *Metropolitan Pulpit*, vol. 18, 263–264.

7. Oswald Chambers, *The Best from All His Books*, Harry Verploegh, ed. (Nashville: Oliver Nelson, 1987), 244.

8. Ibid, 260.

9. Leonard Ravenhill, *Revival God's Way* (Grand Rapids: Bethany House, 1983), 98.